Tyndale Old  Commentaries

Volume 13

TOTC

Esther

Tyndale Old Testament Commentaries

Volume 13

Series Editor: David G. Firth
Consulting Editor: Tremper Longman III

Esther

An Introduction and Commentary

Debra Reid

Inter-Varsity Press

IVP Academic
Evangelically Rooted. Critically Engaged.

INTER-VARSITY PRESS
Norton Street, Nottingham NG7 3HR, England
Website: www.ivpbooks.com
Email: ivp@ivpbooks.com

INTERVARSITY PRESS
PO Box 1400, Downers Grove, Illinois 60515, USA
Website: www.ivpress.com
Email: email@ivpress.com

First published 2008

British Library Cataloguing in Publication Data
A catalogue record for this book is available from the British Library.

UK ISBN: 978-1-84474-244-8

Library of Congress Cataloging-in-Publication Data
These data have been requested.

US ISBN: 978-0-8308-4213-1

Set in Garamond 11/13pt
Typeset in Great Britain by Avocet Typeset, Chilton, Aylesbury, Bucks
Printed and bound in the United States of America

CONTENTS

GENERAL PREFACE

The decision to completely revise the Tyndale Old Testament Commentaries is an indication of the important role that the series has played since its opening volumes were released in the mid-1960s. They represented at that time, and have continued to represent, commentary writing that was committed both to the importance of the text of the Bible as Scripture and a desire to engage with as full a range of interpretative issues as possible without being lost in the minutiae of scholarly debate. The commentaries aimed to explain the biblical text to a generation of readers confronting models of critical scholarship and new discoveries from the Ancient Near East, while remembering that the Old Testament is not simply another text from the ancient world. Although no uniform process of exegesis was required, all the original contributors were united in their conviction that the Old Testament remains the word of God for us today. That the original volumes fulfilled this role is evident from the way in which they continue to be used in so many parts of the world.

A crucial element of the original series was that it should offer an up-to-date reading of the text, and it is precisely for this reason that new volumes are required. The questions confronting readers in the first half of the twenty-first century are not necessarily those from the second half of the twentieth. Discoveries from the Ancient Near East continue to shed new light on the Old Testament, and emphases in exegesis have changed markedly.

Whilst remaining true to the goals of the initial volumes, the need for contemporary study of the text requires that the series as a whole be updated. This updating is not simply a matter of commissioning new volumes to replace the old. We have also taken the opportunity to update the format of the series to reflect a key emphasis from linguistics, which is that texts communicate in larger blocks rather than in shorter segments such as individual verses. Because of this, the treatment of each section of the text includes three segments. First, a short note on *Context* is offered, placing the passage under consideration in its literary setting within the book, as well as noting any historical issues crucial to interpretation. The *Comment* segment then follows the traditional structure of the commentary, offering exegesis of the various components of a passage. Finally, a brief comment is made on *Meaning*, by which is meant the message that the passage seeks to communicate within the book, highlighting its key theological themes. This section brings together the detail of the *Comment* to show how the passage under consideration seeks to communicate as a whole.

Our prayer is that these new volumes will continue the rich heritage of the Tyndale Old Testament Commentaries and that they will continue to witness to the God who is made known in the text.

David G. Firth, Series Editor
Tremper Longman III, Consulting Editor

AUTHOR'S PREFACE

In June 2006, I was privileged to hear the Chief Rabbi, Dr Jonathan Sacks, deliver a lecture entitled 'Living as a biblical people in a secular age'. In his lecture, the Chief Rabbi took the following themes: the importance of rest, learning, community, trust in times of insecurity and uncertainty, and maintaining a sense of destination (our part in the eternal narrative). What an apt summary of the challenge that the book of Esther presents to us today! In the course of this project, I have been surprised again by the present relevance of this ancient story. It is a story written to inspire and challenge us, and to move us to celebrate the moments in our own life stories for which we are truly grateful. I hope you will find time to sit down and read the story of Esther in one sitting. Its meaning is to be found most clearly in its wholeness, although there are significant pointers to that meaning in its individual units. This commentary attempts to give due credit both to the story's literary finesse and to its didactic purpose (hence the introductory section and, in the commentary itself, the employment of the headings 'context', 'comment' and 'meaning'). But, like all stories, its impact remains personal as you relate it to your own unique story. Wherever appropriate, I have used section headings that employ the wording of the biblical text (in inverted commas) in order to emphasize the way in which the divisions I have used rely on emphases within the text itself. Due to its widespread use in churches today, I have used the New

International Version as the basic English translation, quotations from which are given in italics. Other versions have been consulted, and I have indicated where I found their renditions particularly interesting. I should perhaps stress that in a book like Esther, with its careful literary design, many of its design features are hidden in translation, hence the frequent comment on the Hebrew text itself.

I am indebted to many other commentators whose insights have proved invaluable, not least Joyce Baldwin, the writer of the first Tyndale Commentary on Esther. The bibliography lists the works that I have consulted regularly, and I recognize that this Commentary would never have emerged without convenient access to such resources of knowledge and understanding. It is therefore with great gratitude that I record the generous assistance of Mrs Judy Powles, Librarian at Spurgeon's College. I was originally invited to write this commentary by the former Series Editor for the Tyndale Old Testament Commentaries, Dr Martin Selman, who died in December 2004. Having worked with Martin for over seventeen years, I owe much of my own love for the Old Testament to his inspiration, example and encouragement. I am thankful to David Firth, the newly appointed Series Editor, for continuing Martin's legacy by offering me his own patient, insightful and encouraging assistance.

Finally, I record my thanks to all those who have suffered my obsession with Esther over these last two years, including my colleagues at Spurgeon's College, my fellow church members at Horley Baptist Church and my family. Special thanks are reserved for my husband David, who has undertaken more than his fair share of home and family duties recently. I dedicate this book to our three lovely boys, Peter, Matthew and Andrew. I hope Esther's story will inspire them, and that they, with us all, will one day understand their own life stories, whatever twists and turns they may take, as examples of God's intervening and saving activity at work in our world today.

Debra Reid
Spurgeon's College

SELECT BIBLIOGRAPHY

Allen, L. and Laniak, T. (2003), *Ezra, Nehemiah and Esther*, NIBC (Carlisle: Paternoster).

Alter, R. and Kermode, F. (eds.) (1987), *The Literary Guide to the Bible* (Mass.: Harvard University Press).

Anderson, B. W. (1950), 'The Place of the Book of Esther in the Christian Bible', *JR* 30:32–43.

Baldwin, J. G. (1984), *Esther*, Tyndale Old Testament Commentaries (Leicester: IVP).

Barnett, R. D. (1966), *Illustrations of Old Testament History* (London: British Museum).

Bauckham, R. (1989), *The Bible in Politics: How to Read the Bible Politically* (London: SPCK).

— (2002), *Gospel Women: Studies of the Named Women in the Gospels* (Edinburgh: T. & T. Clark).

Bechtel, C. M. (2002), Esther, Interpretation: A Bible Commentary for Teaching and Preaching (Louisville: John Knox Press).

Beckett, M. (2002), *Gospel in Esther* (Carlisle: Paternoster).

Beckwith, R. (1985), *The Old Testament Canon of the New Testament Church* (Grand Rapids: Eerdmans).

Berlin, A. (2001), *Esther*, JPS Bible Commentary (Philadelphia: Jewish Publication Society).

Brenner, A. (ed.) (1995), *A Feminist Companion to Esther, Judith and Susanna* (Sheffield: Sheffield Academic Press).

Brueggemann, W. (2002), 'That the World May be Redescribed', *Interpretation* 56/4: 359–367.

Bush, F. (1996), *Ruth/Esther*, WBC 9 (Dallas: Word Books).

Clines, D. J. A. (1984a), *Ezra, Nehemiah and Esther,* NCBC (Grand Rapids: Eerdmans).

— (1984b), *The Esther Scroll: The Story of the Story*, JSOTSup 30 (Sheffield: Sheffield Academic Press).

— (1990), 'Reading Esther from Left to Right: Contemporary Strategies for Reading a Biblical Text', in W. E. Fowl, D. J. A. Clines, and S. E. Porter, *The Bible in Three Dimensions* (Sheffield: Sheffield Academic Press; JSOTSup 87:31–52).

Coggins, R. J. and Re'emi, S. P. (1985), *Nahum, Obadiah, Esther: Israel among the Nations*, ITC (Grand Rapids: Eerdmans; Edinburgh: Hansel).

Day, L. (1995), *Three Faces of a Queen: Characterization in the Books of Esther* (Sheffield: Sheffield Academic Press; JSOTSup 186).

Day, P. L. (1989), *Gender and Difference in Ancient Israel* (Minneapolis: Fortress).

Dodd, C. H. (1961), *The Parables of the Kingdom* (Glasgow: Fontana Collins).

Dorothy, C. V. (1997), *The Books of Esther: Structural, Genre and Textual Integrity* (Sheffield: Sheffield Academic Press; JSOTSup 187).

Driver, S. R. (1960), *An Introduction to the Literature of the Old Testament* (New York: T. & T. Clark).

Durham, J. I. (1987), *Exodus*, WBC 3 (Waco Texas: Word Books).

Eissfeldt, O. (1965), *The Old Testament: An Introduction* (Oxford: Blackwell).

Firth, D. G. (1997), 'The Book of Esther: A Neglected Paradigm for Dealing with the State', *Old Testament Essays* 10 (1):18–26.

— (2003), 'The Third Quest for the Historical Mordecai and the Genre of the Book of Esther', *Old Testament Essays* 16 (2):233–243.

Fox, M. V. (1983), 'The Structure of the Book of Esther', in *Isac Leo Seeligmann Volume: Essays of the Bible and the Ancient World*, vol. 3 (ed. A. Rofe and Y. Zakovitch, Jerusalem: E. Rubinstein), 291–303.

— (1990), 'The Religion of the Book of Esther', *Judaism* 39 (2):135–147.

— (1991a), *The Redaction of the Book of Esther: On Reading Composite Texts*, SBL monograph 40 (Atlanta: Scholars Press).

— (1991b), *Character and Ideology in the Book of Esther* (University of South Carolina: South Carolina Press; 2nd edn, 2001, Grand Rapids: Eerdmans).

Friedberg, A. D. (2000), 'A New Clue in the Dating of the Composition of the Book of Esther', *VT* 50(4):561–565.

— (2003), 'Dating the Composition of the Book of Esther: A response to Larsson' *VT* 53(3):427–429.

Frolov, S. (2002), 'Two Eunuchs, Two Conspiracies, and One Loyal Jew: The Narrative of Botched Regicide in Esther as Text- and Redaction-Critical Test Case', *VT* 52(3):304–325.

Goldingay, J. (1990), *Approaches to Old Testament Interpretation*, (Leicester: Apollos).

Goldman, S. (1990), 'Narrative and Ethical Ironies in Esther', *JSOT* 47:15–31.

Gordis, R. (1981), 'Religion, Wisdom and History in the Book of Esther – A New Solution to an Old Crux', *JBL* 100(3):359–388.

Greenstein, E. L. (2004), 'A Jewish Reading of Esther', in J. Neusner, B. A. Levine, and E. S. Frerichs (eds.), *Judaic Perspectives on Ancient Israel* (Oregon: Wipf and Stock), 225–243.

Hallo, W. W. (1983), 'The First Purim', *BA* 46(1):19–26.

Heltzer, M. (1992), 'The Book of Esther: Where Does Fiction Start and History End?' *Bible Review* 8:24–30.

Herodotus (c. 445–424 BC), *The Histories of the Persian Wars* (trans. A. de Selincourt, Baltimore, 1968).

Houk, C. B. (2003), 'Syllable-word Patterns in Esther', *ZAW* 115(4):578–585.

Howard, D. M. (1997), 'Theology of Esther', *NIDOTTE* 4:582–585.

Huey, F. B. (1990), 'Irony as the Key to Understanding the Book of Esther', *Southwestern Journal of Theology,* 32:36–39.

Humphreys, W. L. (1973), 'A Life-style for Diaspora: A Study of the Tales of Esther and Daniel', *JBL* 92:211–223.

Jobes, K. H. (1999), *Esther,* NIV Application Commentary (Grand Rapids: Zondervan).

Josephus (1961), *The Life, Against Apion* (London: Heinemann) 1:37–42.

Klein, L. R. (1995), 'Honor and Shame in Esther' in A. Brenner (ed.), *A Feminist Companion to Esther, Judith and Susanna* (Sheffield: Sheffield Academic Press), 149–175.

Kossmann, R. (1999), *Die Esthernovelle*, Brill: VT Supplements 79.

LaCocque, A. (1987), 'Haman in the Book of Esther', *Hebrew Annual Review*, 11: 207–222.

— (1999), 'The Different Versions of Esther', *Biblical Interpretation* 7: 301–322.

Laniak, T. S. (1998), *Shame and Honor in the Book of Esther*, SBL Dissertation Series 165 (Atlanta: Scholars Press).

Larsson, G. (2002), 'Is the Book of Esther Older than Has Been Believed?', *VT* 52 (1):130–131.

Levenson, J. D. (1997), *Esther*, Old Testament Library (Louisville: Westminster John Knox Press).

Lockyer, H. (1961), *All the Kings and Queens of the Bible* (Grand Rapids: Zondervan).

Long, G. (1999), 'The Written Story: Towards Understanding Text as Representation and Function', *VT* 49(2): 165–185.

Lubitch, R. (1993), 'A Feminist's Look at Esther', *Judaism*, 42(4): 438–446.

Miller, C. H. (1980), 'Esther's Levels of Meaning', *ZAW*, 92:145–148.

Moore, C. A. (1971), *Esther*, The Anchor Bible (New York: Doubleday).

— (1975), 'Archaeology and the Book of Esther', *BA* 38:62–79.

— (1987), 'Eight Questions Most Frequently Asked About the Book of Esther', *Bible Review* 3:16–32.

Müller, M. (1996), *The First Bible of the Church: A Plea for the Septuagint*, Sheffield: *JSOT* 206.

Neusner, J. (1983), *Midrash in Context* (Philadelphia: Fortress Press).

— (1988), *The Mishnah: A New Translation* (New Haven: Yale University Press).

O'Keefe, R. A. (2005), 'Critical Remarks on Houk's "Statistical Analysis of Genesis Sources"', *JSOT* 29(4), 409–437.

Pfeiffer, R. H. (1948), *Introduction to the Old Testament* (New York: Harper).

Reid, D. (2000), *Ruth and Esther* (Leicester: Crossway Books).

Sandmel, S. (1978), *The Hebrew Scriptures* (New York: Oxford University Press).

Sedgwick, C. (2003), 'God is Working His Purpose Out', *ET* 114(11): 381–382.

Selman, M. J. (1994), *1 and 2 Chronicles*, Tyndale Old Testament Commentaries (Leicester: IVP).

Sundberg, A. (1958), *The Old Testament of the Early Church*, HTS 20 (Cambridge Mass.).

Talmon, S. (1963), 'Wisdom in the Book of Esther', *VT* 13, 419–455.

— (1995), 'Was the Book of Esther Known at Qumran?' *DSD* 2 (3), 249–267.

Tov, E. (1982), 'The Lucianic Text of the Canonical and the Apocryphal Section of Esther: A Rewritten Biblical Book', *Textus* 10, 1–25.

Walfish, B. D. (1993), *Esther in Medieval Garb: Jewish Interpretations of the Book of Esther in the Middle Ages* (Albany: SUNY Press).

Weisman, Z. (1998), *Political Satire in the Book of Esther* (Atlanta: Scholars Press).

Wills, L. M. (1990), *The Jew in the Court of the Foreign King: Ancient Jewish Court Legends* (Minneapolis: Fortress).

White, S. A. (1989), 'A Feminine Model for Jewish Diaspora', *Gender and Difference in Ancient Israel*, ed. P. Day, Minneapolis:161–177.

Whybray, R. Norman (2002), *The Good Life in the Old Testament* (Edinburgh: T. & T. Clark).

Yamauchi, E. M. (1990), *Persia and the Bible* (Grand Rapids: Baker Books).

ABBREVIATIONS

BA	*Biblical Archaeologist*
BHS	Biblia Hebraica Stuttgartensia (ed. K. Elliger and W. Rudolf, Stuttgart, 1969–1975, 1984³)
CHJ. I	Cambridge History of Judaism, vol. I, ed. W. D. Davies and Louis Finkelstein (Cambridge: Cambridge University Press, 1984)
DSD	*Dead Sea Discoveries*
ET	*Expository Times*
GK	Gesenius' Hebrew Grammar, (ed. E. Kautzch, Oxford: Clarendon Press, 1910)
HTS	Harvard Theological Studies
ITC	International Theological Commentary
JBL	*Journal of Biblical Literature*
JR	*Journal of Religion*
JSOT	*Journal for the Study of the Old Testament*
JSOTSup	Journal for the Study of the Old Testament Supplement Series
NCBC	*New Century Bible Commentary*
NIDOTTE	*New International Dictionary of Old Testament Theology and Exegesis*
SBL	Society of Biblical Literature
VT	*Vetus Testamentum*
WBC	Word Biblical Commentary
ZAW	*Zeitschrift für die Alttestamentliche Wissenschaft*

Texts and versions

KJV	King James' Version
LXX	Septuagint
MT	Masoretic Text
NIV	New International Version
NRSV	New Revised Standard Version
RSV	Revised Standard Version
NKJV	New King James' Version
TNIV	Today's New International Version

INTRODUCTION

1. The nature of the book of Esther

What kind of book is Esther? It is this question that taunts us as we try to understand the significance of this short OT book. On the one hand it appears to be a simple historical account. On the other it is a carefully crafted piece of literary genius. From one perspective, its main focus is upon the individual who gives the book its name; from another the spotlight is on a whole nation. Thematically and stylistically there is both simplicity and complexity, a transparency that is mixed with intrigue. Theologically there are obvious implications of the story, but there is also mystery and dilemma. Ethically, good triumphs over evil, but does the end justify the means along the way? Is the book relevant or irrelevant? Is it to be enjoyed at a surface level or penetrated for its hidden depths? Is it meant to convey historical facts, or is its meaning to be found in application to our lives? Is its value for one nation or many, or for individual people? What is the *raison d'être* of the book of Esther?

These questions are reminiscent of those we sometimes pose of the parables of Jesus. We are fully aware that a full explanation of their details and their meaning somehow escapes us. The New Testament scholar C. H. Dodd claims that the parables 'leave us in sufficient doubt about their precise application in order to tease our minds into active thought' (1961: 16). This is at least part of Esther's compelling quality. The story taunts and teases us. As soon as we think we are beginning to understand its themes or its literary features, we become alert to our own dissatisfaction with our perception. But rather than being deterred, we become more absorbed. Take, for example, the fact that God's name is never mentioned in the text. Instead of giving up on a theological quest, we find ourselves searching more earnestly for a God whose non-appearance seems to enhance his presence. The result is that, because our minds are teased, our subsequent theological conclusions incorporate reflection at a number of penetrating and intriguing levels.

This, of course, is similar to our responses to personal testimonies about journeys of faith. Testimonies are our life stories – how life began for us, how we came to experience salvation through Christ, how life has continued for us. It is my contention that the value and meaning of the book of Esther lies in its testimonial value. In this book we read of Esther's early life (living with her uncle in the Persian Empire). We read what life is like for Esther when she encounters deliverance and salvation (her unenviable position in the king's palace), and her active acceptance of her own role within these processes (*for such a time as this*, Esth. 4:14). The story is concluded by the description of what life is like for Esther after this particular event of deliverance, but somehow it is a story that remains ongoing and is open-ended. Another way of reading the story is to understand that it represents the testimony not of Esther alone but of her people together. This adds further significance to the references to the establishment of the Purim festival at the end of the book. Life now will never be the same for Esther's people. An encounter with salvation always has lasting and wide-ranging effects, encompassing its original participants as well as those to whom the testimony is conveyed. This, after all, is Scripture, and Scripture is a document of faith, the story of salvation – history that deserves to be heard and that teases its every hearer into active thought as well as personal and corporate reflection.

2. Origin and date

The book of Esther clearly emerged within the general time band between 465 BC (the end of the reign of Ahasuerus) and AD 70 (when Josephus made full use of the story in his *Antiquities*).[1] The question is, can this time band be narrowed further? The earliest date would allow the author to be a contemporary of the events described which occurred immediately following Ahasuerus' reign. Esther 1:1 may imply that time has elapsed since Ahasuerus' reign, and therefore the events described would have happened in the reign of Artaxerxes (464–423 BC). If this is indeed the implication, then a late fifth-century *terminus a quo* is established. It seems that the book reflects a Persian setting (the Persian period lasting from Cyrus' capture of Babylon in 539 BC until Alexander captured Tyre in 333/2 BC) but this does not mean that the final form of the book was settled during this era.[2]

A look at the internal evidence has led many to conclude that a third-century Hellenistic date of writing is probable.[3] To support this argument scholars have drawn on the evidence of the second-century BC Qumran Scrolls, which seem to present a Hebrew language later than that found in the book of Esther.[4] Having

---

1. The Greek additions suggest that Esther was translated into Greek by Lysimachus, by the fourth year of Ptolemy and Cleopatra. If this claim is accurate, then the *terminus ad quem* can be pushed back to 112 BC or 76 BC, depending on whether Ptolemy VIII or Ptolemy XII is intended.

2. For example, it is possible that the book was written in the fifth century BC, even if it reached its final form in the third/second century BC.

3. See, for example, Michael Fox who concludes that Esther would not refer to the 127 satrapies of Persia if the Persian Empire still existed (1991: 139).

4. Shemaryahu Talmon (1995: 249–267) has argued that phrases from Esther are alluded to in the Qumran Scrolls, so the book must have been known by the community, even if it was not preserved by them.

established a pre-second-century dating for Esther on the basis of the diction, idiom and syntax of the Hebrew text, Driver (1960: 484, followed by many others) settled on a third-century date.

But this traditional date has not been universally accepted. Recently, importance has been assigned to the dating formulas within the book of Esther itself. Friedberg argues that these formulas lead to the probability that Esther was written at a much earlier date. He asserts that the post-exilic books show a development in dating formulas, moving away from the traditional numerical system (where months are not given names but referred to by numerals, beginning at spring time), to the complete adoption of the Babylonian system of names for months (i.e. month 1 becomes Nisan etc) – a process that is complete in Ezra-Nehemiah (second half of the fourth century). Friedberg shows that Esther lies in the middle of this post-exilic process, because it uses mixed formulas, indicating that the process to full use of the Babylonian system had begun but was not completed, and therefore concludes that a late fifth-century date for Esther is most probable.[5]

It seems that at least the possibility of a late fifth-century date for Esther has been established. Furthermore, it is likely that Esther was written within the Persian period, not least because the story is most meaningful within that setting, and the absence of reference to Hellenistic culture supports this. This reduces the time band for Esther to between late fifth century and the first half of the fourth century BC, a time span consistent with the internal and linguistic evidence within the book itself.[6]

3. Historical background and setting

While questions about the historical reliability of the Esther story will be addressed in a later section (p. 30), it is necessary here to

---

5. Friedberg (2000: 561–565) lays out the details of his argument and a response has been made by Larsson (2002: 130–131). Friedberg (2003: 427–429) has replied to support his case.

6. Note that this conclusion marks a return to the view of Baldwin (1984: 48–49), which has generally been abandoned in the intervening years.

consider the historical setting in which this story emerges.

The origin of this book, by virtue of its dating, language and thematic content, is firmly fixed within the Persian Empire governed by the Achaemenid kings. Between 545 and 538 BC, the Achaemenid kings conquered the whole of the Middle East (including Palestine) and had established the largest of all the empires in the ancient world. Cyrus (559–530 BC) was particularly responsible for the extension of the Empire's borders, and although his military advances were quite conclusive, even ruthless, he treated people within his Empire with respect, seeing himself as their liberator rather than a tyrant. Cyrus (who is portrayed as the servant of the Lord in Isaiah 45) allowed the Jewish people to return to Palestine at the end of the Babylonian exile (539 BC) in order to rebuild the temple. Cyrus was followed by Cambyses II (530–522 BC), who spent much of his time occupied with advances into Egypt, and then by Darius (522–486 BC). During this time, the Empire's power was consolidated, despite internal power struggles (Darius' ascension was by no means straightforward), and administrative structures were developed, including the division of the Empire into satrapies and smaller sub-provinces. Darius was also responsible for the palace complex built at Susa (the ancient capital of Elam, modern-day Iran). After Darius came Xerxes (Ahasuerus, 486–465 BC) in whose reign the story of Esther is set (Esth. 1:1), and then Artaxerxes I (464–423 BC) in whose reign the first version of the story probably emerged.

This period was dominated by territorial concerns and intellectual advances. Xerxes himself lost strategic battles with the Greeks at a time when Greek culture flourished in Athens with the emergence of Socrates, Pericles and Pythagorus. Our main evidence about this era comes from Herodotus, the Greek historian, whose *Histories of the Persian Wars* (490–480 BC) tell us about the Persian kings and their campaigns. Although we must be cautious about the reliability of Herodotus' accounts (he was after all a Greek writer whose allegiance to the Greek people would have made him an enemy of the Persian Empire), his writings do bear evidence to Persian personalities and practice. For example, Herodotus describes Xerxes as tall and handsome, an ambitious ruler and warrior. It appears that Herodotus was quite fascinated by Xerxes, because about a third of his history book is taken up with his reign. Further information about Xerxes is available in the Behistun Inscription of Darius that contains the Persian records of the Empire. Here Xerxes is portrayed as a successful ruler who quelled revolts in Babylon and Egypt – certainly in Babylon he ordered hard penalties, not least the destruction of the temple and statue of the Babylonian god Marduk.

So the story of Esther finds its meaning within such a setting. It concerns the fate of a group of Jews, who, about fifty or sixty years after being allowed to return to Jerusalem, still found themselves in the eastern Persian Empire. Their situation was not easy. While some Jews clearly rose to prominence (compare the evidence in the book of Daniel), the kings were lenient towards them only to a point, and any hint of subversive activity was treated ruthlessly. This volatile situation lies behind the drama of the Esther story – for its first readers the tension would need no explanation. To this, the religious tension needs to be added. We know that Xerxes completed the palace at Persepolis, in honour of himself and the Zoroastrian god Ahuramazda (having removed the worship of Daiva, the old Iranian god).[7] To a king who made religious concerns his business, the Jewish population with their own religion and customs would be viewed as particularly troublesome. Against such a background, was there any hope for God's people? It is therefore the historical setting of this story that imbibes it with theological meaning.

4. Canonical status

The acceptance of Esther into the OT canon was not straightforward. To some extent, our knowledge of the process raises as many questions as it provides answers.

The process of the establishment of the canon of the OT as a whole is itself problematic. There is no widespread agreement about when the OT canon was finally agreed, or the timing of steps towards

---

7. For further details of the evidence from the Daiva Inscription of Xerxes, see CHJ. I: 293.

it. Most scholars concur that the Jewish canon reached a point of closure some time between 200 BC and AD 200.[8] Prior to the second century AD, most of our information about the canon's development comes from three Jewish sources: evidence from Qumran (150 BC – AD 70), Josephus (AD 90), and the early rabbinical writings. These sources give clues about Esther's early place within the OT canon:

(i)   *Qumran*: Esther is the only book of our present OT canon that is not found among the Qumran Scrolls. While it has been argued that this suggests Esther did not enjoy early acceptance, it could equally be because the Essene community did not celebrate the festival of Purim, and therefore its omission from the Scrolls is to be expected. It would have been surplus to requirements.[9]

(ii)   *Josephus*: Reliance on the evidence of Josephus does not take us much further in our appraisal of Esther's canonicity. Josephus states that there are twenty-two OT books, thirteen of which record the history of Israel from the death of Moses until Artaxerxes. In neither case does Josephus name the books that make up the numbers cited. While the very mention of Artaxerxes suggests Josephus knew Esther, this cannot be proved beyond reasonable doubt.[10] What Josephus' evidence does suggest is that the concept of canon existed at this time, even if diversity within Judaism allowed for non-universal canons.

(iii) *Early rabbinical evidence*: There is limited evidence that a council

---

8. For a summary of the issues relating to the formation of the canon, see Goldingay, 1990: 138–145. Note that Goldingay argues that canon establishment should not be linked to the synod at Jamnia (AD 90), because the status of this synod and the precise meaning and value of its canonical decisions are themselves debatable. See also Sundberg 1958: 113–128 and Sandmel 1978: 14.

9. Shemaryahu Talmon (1995: 249–267) argues that the Qumran Scrolls allude to Esther, suggesting that the story was known to, even if not preserved by, the community.

10. See Josephus, *Against Apion*, I: 37–43.

in Jamnia (Palestine) in AD 90 decided that Esther should be accepted.[11] The Mishnah (assembled in the first two centuries AD) gives directions about how the 'Book of Purim' should be read, suggesting Esther's place had been established in the canon at least by the end of the second century. The Mishnah is important because 'it forms the foundation for the Babylonian and Palestinian Talmuds. It therefore stands alongside the Hebrew Bible as the holy book upon which the Judaism of the past nineteen hundred years is constructed'.[12]

It is possible that the Palestinian Talmud implies that Esther's canonicity was disputed as early as the second century on the basis that it advocates a festival not instituted in the Pentateuch.[13] Furthermore, Rabbi Samuel (third century AD) is cited as the source of a claim that Esther was not a sacred book.[14] Finally assembled in the fifth or sixth centuries AD, the Midrash (a book containing collections of exegetical studies) contains commentary on Esther (along with the Pentateuch, Lamentations, Songs and Ruth). There are two relevant Midrashim: Esther Rabbah 1 (which expounds Esth. 1 and 2) and Esther Rabbah 2 (which expounds Esth. 3:1 – 8:15).[15]

---

11. But see footnote 8, above.
12. See Neusner (1988: xv). The instructions concerning Esther come in the tenth subdivision entitled megillah of the second division of the Mishnah dealing with moed (appointed times). The entry deals with when Purim should be celebrated, where and how the Scrolls of Esther should be read and who should read them. It concludes with discussion about the offerings and Torah readings that accompanied the festival (see Neusner's translation, 1988: 316–324).
13. Megilla 70d affirms that only Mosaic laws and festivals should be observed by Jews.
14. The evidence comes from Megilla 7a (Babylonian Talmud), which refers to Rab Judah recalling the comments of Samuel that Esther does not make the hands unclean.
15. It is usually agreed that Esther Rabbah 1 was redacted at the start of the sixth century (drawing on Aquila's translation), and Esther Rabbah 2 in the eleventh century (making use of the Septuagint Additions).

The interpretation of this evidence is varied. While it may imply a reluctance to accept this book, it may alternatively suggest that interest in Esther, and its distinctive nature, was aroused from the outset. Certainly if we accept an early date for the establishment of the OT canon, then the rabbinical debates concern a book already established in the canon (and questioned by a minority), rather than a book seeking to make an entry (and questioned by the majority). Indeed, the canonicity of Esther is rarely a matter of debate after the first four centuries AD, and it has been argued that Esther became one of the most important books outside the Pentateuch in later Jewish circles.[16]

Christian sources provide some further information. Early evidence comes from Melito (Bishop of Sardis), who in AD 170 omits Esther from his list of canonical books (which otherwise reflects the present canon). In the writings of the early Church Fathers, there is silence in both commentating and referring to Esther. But Esther was affirmed by the church councils of Hippo (AD 393) and Carthage (AD 397), and at this point the Christian church considered the canon of the whole Bible to be established. Prior to this, Beckwith (1985: 296–297) suggests that there was a split between the Eastern church, where Esther's canonicity was questioned (for example, in the fourth centuries by Athanasius, Gregory of Nazianzus, Theodore of Mopsuestia) and the Western church, where Esther was widely accepted.

The evidence is obviously inconclusive, but it should be remem-

---

16. Beckwith (1985: 291–292) suggests that this view is supported by the Cairo Genizah, where fragments from Esther are more numerous than any other book outside the Pentateuch. This view is disputed by researchers at the Cairo Institute at Cambridge, who suggest that fragments of Esther do not outnumber those of other OT books. The present writer, however, notes that Esther's appearance in medieval Jewish rabbinical literature is sporadic. (See Debra K. Reid, 'The Fragments of the Commentary on Isaiah by Saadya Gaon ben Josef Al-Fayyoumi', appendix 5, pp. 490–502 , unpublished thesis, 1991. This Commentary quotes liberally from OT books [601 quotations from 35 books] but there is no use of Esther.)

bered that the distinctive content and character of Esther might itself account for uncertainty about its status.

Over the centuries there has always been interest in Esther. We know that in the early Middle Ages Rhabanus Maurus (Bishop of Mainz, ninth century) wrote a commentary on Esther. Luther (*Table Talk*, 1914; see Laniak, 1998) seemed to dislike the book of Esther and accused the story of impropriety and excessive Judaizing. Even today modern scholars make similar complaints, adding to Esther's sins that of gratuitous violence (see Pfeiffer 1948, Eissfeldt 1965 and even the Jewish scholar, Sandmel 1978).

However, the book of Esther remains central to Jewish festival liturgy, and Christian theologians today appreciate its historical progress into the canon as a sign of its centrality and importance within the faith story of God's people.

Position within the canon

In Hebrew manuscripts, Esther is usually positioned as the last of the five scrolls (*mĕgillôt*). These books (Song of Songs, Ruth, Lamentations, Ecclesiastes and Esther) are read at the five major festivals of the Jewish year and were given the collective label 'Scrolls' by the tenth-century Tiberian Masoretes. In BHS these Scrolls follow Job and precede Daniel in the third section of the OT, the 'Writings' (*kĕtûbîm*), which follow 'Law' (*tôrâ*) and 'Prophets' (*nĕbî'îm*).[17]

The Christian Bible places Esther as the last of seventeen books of sacred history. It opens with the formula *wyhy* (*'and it happened'*), typical of the history books (cf. e.g. Joshua, Judges, Samuel and

---

17. The order of the Scrolls is related to the order of the Jewish festivals at which each scroll is read, beginning with the spring new year: Song of Songs is read at Passover (April); Ruth at Shavuot (May–June); Lamentations on ninth of Av (July–August); Ecclesiastes at Sukkot (September–October); and Esther at Purim (March). Other Hebrew canons bear evidence to a differing ordering of the OT books. Sometimes the megilloth do not appear as a group (e.g. Ruth appears with the historical books, Esther sometimes follows Daniel and precedes Ezra–Nehemiah and Chronicles).

Ezra). This means that the Christian Bible no longer places the five Scrolls *(mĕgillôt)* together. In fact, over the years, Esther's position in the Christian Bible has been variable (for example, it has also appeared at the very end of the OT canon, possibly reflecting the view that it was the last book to find its place within the OT canon).

Relationship to the rest of the canon

Thematically Esther has a number of connections with other material within the OT. Indeed, it is possible that its position in the Hebrew canon is connected to its theme. For example, the hope and celebration in Esther contrasts with and replaces the despair and mourning of Lamentations. Esther also connects with Daniel (which follows the *mĕgillôt*), as both share a similar setting and plot, focusing on Jews prospering in a foreign land. The most obvious connections with other OT books relate to the emphasis that God's people have a history and future because of God's intervention. Thematic overlap exists with the stories of Joseph's exploits in Genesis and more generally with the book of Exodus. With a more individual focus, Job and Ruth also investigate the theological theme of the apparent absence of God in the life of his people.

When it comes to Esther's relationship with the NT canon, we are confronted with the fact that Esther (along with Ecclesiastes and Song of Solomon) is not cited in the NT. However, recent studies by Beckett (2002) and Jobes (1999) have re-emphasized the possibility of typological interpretations of Esther (renewing some medieval approaches), even suggesting the possibility of Esther representing a type of Christ as servant of the Lord.

Esther has many parallels with the apocryphal book of Judith. Judith means 'Jewess', which in turn implies devotion to her nation's cause. Written c.150 BC, the book tells the story of Judith, a beautiful woman, who causes the downfall of Nebuchadnezzar's chief general. Like Esther, the hopeful theme is that God will deliver weak people who trust him.

Other connections to the Apocrypha relate to the Greek additions of 106 verses that have a reverential tone and exalt God's righteousness (see Appendix).

5. Literary issues

Since the 1980s, the literary features of the book of Esther have received scrutiny. It has been recognized that it is impossible to determine the message of the book without paying due respect to the medium of that message, the written text itself. The features of the text, and the style adopted by the author, give us clues about the writer's approach and message. The writer's choices in terms of emphasis, mood, tone, structure and language, reveal something of the central theme and purpose.

On a surface reading, the book of Esther is clearly a narrative. It tells a story and invites its readers to witness the unfolding drama. The story is given a historical setting but contains evidence of descriptive poetic licence and creativity. The story-line is clear and accessible. It has a beginning, middle, and end. Its basic elements are not complicated but its characters are as intriguing as they are straightforward. The reader quickly becomes aware of the author's own evaluation of the rights and wrongs of the events, and the reader's own sympathy is evoked. In other words, Esther is a good short story, a sound piece of literature, an attractive literary unit. But, however satisfying a surface reading is, by probing its literary features we access the writer's meaning and purpose and can interpret the text in such light. Because we are looking at a canonical text, this interpretative task is always the goal of our study rather than the pure literary pursuit, but the latter enables the former to be pursued with more confidence.

i. Genre

The struggle to identify literary genre is the struggle to apply a label to the text as a whole. It's all about asking the question, 'what sort of literature is this?' In the case of Esther, numerous solutions are proposed. Esther has been described as conforming to many literary types. These seem to fall into the following main categories:

(a) Esther is non-fictional narrative (historical narrative or historical novel). By calling Esther a historical narrative, it implies that the book contains an accurate account of a series of events that took place at the stated time and place. Particular attention is paid to the historical features of the text and the historical framework of the

narrative, and the conclusion is that the primary purpose of the book is to record history accurately.

The label 'historical novel' has similar but not identical implications. This genre allows for the recognition of the historical setting of the book, while also recognizing the literary creativity that the writer employs. In other words, the author is writing about history, but with a degree of poetic licence. So the writer has historical interests but also literary interests. Something of historical importance is being told, but in a creative way. Every detail serves either historical or literary interests, but we need to determine which. Understanding Esther as a historical novel does not deny the importance of history in Jewish and Christian faith; instead it underlines it. The writer is keen to record history in a memorable and interesting way, in order to stimulate identification with the unfolding drama and to remind the readers of their place in the continued line of God's interaction with his people.[18]

A historical reading of the Esther story seems coherent with the writer's own intentions, for there are no indications in the text itself that the foundational events of the story are make-believe.[19]

(b) Esther is a fictional narrative (novella, Hellenistic novella, Diaspora novel). Understanding Esther as a fictional narrative allows us to view the book primarily as a creative short story. The story is enhanced by its assigned historical setting, but its setting is not indicative of its historicity. In other words, the story was written for purposes other than historical ones. For example, it could be argued that Esther was written for didactic purposes – to give God's people hope during the Diaspora or to teach them about his faithfulness even when overwhelming odds seem stacked against them.[20] The label 'novella' is used of short novels or long

---

18. See Jobes, 'Telling history in the form of a story may be an unfamiliar approach by modern standards, but it is perhaps a particularly appropriate way for biblical truth to be told' (1999: 32).

19. See Firth (2003) for a discussion of genre issues in relation to history and archaeology.

20. Note that the similar category 'Diaspora story' does not necessarily imply fictional status. Historical events might also serve didactic

stories and has been applied to Esther. Some prefer the title 'Hellenistic novella' in an attempt to parallel Esther with the Hellenistic romance tales.[21] By understanding Esther in this way, the story is viewed as fictional – a story created for its meaning, a fable perhaps.

(c) Esther follows other contemporary literature forms (Persian chronicle, Greek romance, carnival tale, festival aetiology). There have been many attempts to link the genre of Esther with other known contemporary genres. These labels normally imply something about the historicity of the book. For example, if we agree that Esther is written as a Persian court chronicle (or historical annal), then its adopted genre underlines its historical intentions.[22] Similarly, if Esther mirrors Greek romance novellae, its fictional nature is acknowledged by the form it borrows. To understand Esther as a carnival tale or festival aetiology is to suggest that the writer's intention specifically focused on the needs of the Jewish community, by regulating and explaining the carnival/festival of Purim.

The interesting feature about these genres and their application to Esther is that each does have parallels with specific parts of the Esther story, but none seems to be applicable to the text as a whole. This has led some critics to suggest that the text of Esther combines various shorter texts of different genres and origin.

---

purposes, and this is of course the focus of Purim – a celebration of events that the Jews understood had happened and which would always teach them about God's protection and deliverance.

21. For a more detailed discussion, see Fox (1991: 144–147). However, Fox argues that Esther is a short story, so 'story' is a better term than novella anyway (p. 146). Wills (1990: 152–191) argues that an original court legend about Mordecai and Haman has been expanded to form a novella.

22. For further discussion about Persian chronicles and their relationship to Esther, see Gordis (1981: 359–388). Gordis suggests that 'The Book of Esther represents a unique genre in the Hebrew Bible – ostensibly a royal chronicle by a Gentile scribe at the Persian court' (p. 378). Far from undermining its historicity, Gordis argues that Esther is a traditional 'chronicle' reworking of what may be a real historical incident. But compare Fox's attack on Gordis' theory (Fox, 1991: 144).

Alternatively, we might simply accept that the writer of the Esther story relied not on different sources but rather on different literary forms, without slavishly adopting them. So, for example, while the text of Esther may mirror Greek novels in structure and form, the romance and adventure elements so common in this genre are absent in Esther.

(d) Esther follows other biblical literary forms (wisdom tale, narratized lament). It has been long recognized that Esther contains elements of the outlook that characterizes wisdom literature. In particular, the *ad hoc* mentality, lack of historical depth and underdeveloped characterization are proposed as shared features.[23] Similar commonality has been found between the Esther and Joseph narratives – in particular, the fact that the reversal of fortunes motif is prominent in both. Other similarities have been noted between the practical focus of Proverbs and the pragmatic wisdom of Esther. The underlying assumption of Job that righteousness leads to well-being and wrong-doing to disaster is also mirrored in the plot of Esther as Haman falls and Esther rises. Laniak's work comparing Esther with the laments of the Psalms is particularly fruitful. Laniak suggests that understanding Esther as a type of narratized lament, based on the poetic lament structures of the Psalms, provides potential for inter-textual readings. In particular, he draws out the significance of the four 'movements' of biblical laments: crisis, period of abandonment, reversal, state of favour (Allen and Laniak, 2003: 171).

(e) Esther is a unique literary form (burlesque, comedy tale). Even on a surface reading the comical elements in Esther are striking. The portrayals of Ahasuerus and Haman as buffoon and megalomaniac respectively, the amusing coincidences, parallels and reversals, and the mockery and ironic exaggeration are common indulgences of the text, which betray comical intentions. Adele Berlin (2001: xix) suggests that Esther is a particular type of comedy tale – 'burlesque'. This term distinguishes Esther from satirical forms of comedy, because its purpose is entertainment (or creating the 'feel-good' factor) not

---

23. See S. Talmon (1963: 431–433), but note that Niditch (in Brenner, 1995: 44) cautions that these characteristics are also those of folklore texts.

critique. As burlesque, Esther naturally incorporates a tone of mock dignity, exaggerated descriptions, a series of ludicrous coincidences, underdeveloped characters and caricatures, and universal reversals. This does not deny that there is a deeper message in Esther, but means that the features and meaning of that message are understood only if the comic qualities of its genre are recognized.

In the end it is perhaps wise to agree with Laniak (1998: 169) that 'Esther is a text in which the cross-fertilization of various genres should be appreciated.' In many ways Esther is unique within biblical literature, and its uniqueness is recognized by the sheer number of suggestions about its genre. To interpret the text appropriately it is advisable not to put the text in a genre straitjacket, but to be alert to the plethora of possibilities. To a certain extent the genre-quest is self-validating. Even though it may not yield a definitive answer, the search highlights a range of interpretative possibilities that allow us to penetrate beneath the surface reading of the text.

ii. Structure

Various understandings of the structure of the Esther narrative have been proposed. The very existence of numerous approaches underlines the growing acceptance that meaning cannot be separated from form when it comes to text analysis. For this reason, structural analysis is both critical and dangerous. It is dangerous because we may give too much credit to our structural conclusions, which may in turn distract from the text's meanings; it is critical because without it we may miss vital clues about the text's meaning. Fox (1983: 292) works with this perspective in mind and begins his analysis of Esther's structure by stating, 'The purpose of this study is to show how Esther's literary architecture expresses the author's world-view and even hints at his theological viewpoint.' For Fox the 'guiding principle' of the structure of Esther is the theme of reversal,[24] based on the phrase in Esther 9:1, 'now the tables were turned'. This verse itself interprets the events of the story – it is a summary statement emphasizing that events have taken an unex-

---

24. Or more precisely 'peripety' (a term which means a sudden or violent change or reversal, especially in drama).

pected and complete turnaround. The resulting structural analysis is one based on thesis and antithesis (see page 36).[25]

As the text's own interpretation (evidenced by 9:1) demonstrates, the status of the reversal theme in the story's structure must be taken seriously. In Esther this reversal motif has providence at the centre: the reversal occurs because actions of powerful people are overturned by similar actions from a different power source. Although God's name is never mentioned, the implication is that such power and providence can only be divine.[26]

An alternative interpretation of the design of Esther is centred on the place of the Hebrew word *mišteh* in the narrative. This word is translated as 'feast' or 'banquet', and occurs nearly as many times in Esther as it does in the rest of the Old Testament books put together. In Esther, the story is both introduced and concluded by the theme, and the motif supports the main action. In this way, the feast motif serves to establish a satisfying literary quality that cannot be ignored – for there is something aesthetically pleasing about reading a story with this balancing and unifying feature.

These two structural interpretations can be brought together in a way that enhances our appreciation of the text's architectural meaning. It is possible that these two literary themes, reversal and feasting, themselves reflect an overriding motif, the interface between God's providence and human behaviour. This, after all, is one way of interpreting the significance and centrality of Esther in the story. Esther herself is subject to the forces of human behaviour and God's providence as they meet in her lifetime. As human behaviour is reflected in the series of feasts, God's providence is

---

25. Adapted from Fox (1983: 294–296). In this scheme chapters 1 and 2 are seen as preparatory, 6:9 as pivotal, and chapter 9 is interpretative.

26. Fox compares this with examples of peripety in biblical wisdom literature, where God is often not mentioned, but the outcome nonetheless requires the interpretation that execution of recompense or reversal is the natural form that divine justice assumes (1983: 302). Jobes (1999: 41) argues that there is no other reasonable interpretation: 'Because this story is in the canon of the Jews and subsequently the Christians, it is proper to construe that unseen power as God.'

Thesis	Antithesis
3:1	10:3
King Xerxes honoured Haman … giving him a seat of honour higher than that of all other nobles.	Mordecai the Jew was second in rank to King Xerxes, pre-eminent among the Jews …
3:10	8:2a
So the king took his signet ring from his finger and gave it to Haman …	The king took off his signet ring, which he had reclaimed from Haman, and presented it to Mordecai.
3:12	8:9–10a
Then on the thirteenth day of the first month the royal secretaries were summoned. They wrote out in the script of each province and in the language of each people all Haman's orders to the king's satraps, the governors of the various provinces and the nobles of the various peoples. These were written in the name of King Xerxes himself and sealed with his own ring.	At once the royal secretaries were summoned – on the twenty-third day of the third month, the month of Sivan. They wrote out all Mordecai's orders to the Jews, and to the satraps, governors and nobles of the 127 provinces stretching from India to Cush. These orders were written in the script of each province and the language of each people and also to the Jews in their own script and language. Mordecai wrote in the name of King Xerxes, sealed the dispatches with the king's signet ring …
3:13	8:10b–12
Dispatches were sent by couriers to all the king's provinces with the order to destroy, kill and annihilate all the Jews – young and old, women and little children – on a single day, the thirteenth day of the twelfth month, the month of Adar, and to plunder their goods.	… and sent them by mounted couriers, who rode fast horses especially bred for the king. The king's edict granted the Jews in every city the right to assemble and protect themselves; to destroy, kill and annihilate any armed force of any nationality or province that might attack them and their women and children; and to plunder the property of their enemies. The day appointed … was the thirteenth day of the twelfth month, the month of Adar.
3:14	8:13
A copy of the text of the edict was to be issued as law in every province and made known to the people of every nationality so that they would be ready for that day.	A copy of the text of the edict was to be issued as law in every province and made known to the people of every nationality so that the Jews would be ready on that day to avenge themselves on their enemies.
3:15	8:14, 15b
Spurred on by the king's command, the couriers went out, and the edict was issued in the citadel of Susa. The king and Haman sat down to drink, but the city of Susa was bewildered.	The couriers, riding the royal horses, raced out, spurred on by the king's command. And the edict was also issued in the citadel of Susa … And the city of Susa held a joyous celebration.
4:1	8:15a
When Mordecai learned of all that had been done, he tore his clothes, put on sackcloth and ashes, and went out into the city, wailing loudly and bitterly.	Mordecai left the king's presence wearing royal garments of blue and white, a large crown of gold and a purple robe of fine linen.
4:3	8:17a
In every province to which the edict and order of the king came, there was great mourning among the Jews, with fasting, weeping and wailing. Many lay in sackcloth and ashes.	In every province and every city, wherever the edict of the king went, there was joy and gladness among the Jews, with feasting and celebrating.
5:14a	6:13b–14
His wife Zeresh and all his friends said to him, 'Have a gallows built, seventy-five feet high, and ask the king in the morning to have Mordecai hanged on it. Then go with the king to the dinner and be happy.'	His advisers and his wife Zeresh said to him, 'Since Mordecai, before whom your downfall has started, is of Jewish origin, you cannot stand against him – you will surely come to ruin!' While they were still talking with him, the king's eunuchs arrived and hurried Haman away to the banquet Esther had prepared.
6:6–9	6:10
(Haman thinks he is to be honoured and designs an honouring ceremony.)	(Mordecai receives the honour Haman had designed.)

reflected in the reversal of fortunes, which Esther's actions enable her people to experience and celebrate in renewed feasting. The journey of God's people is one of varied emotions: their lack of par-ticipation in the festivities of Ahasuerus' court turns into full participation in the grief caused by his court's decisions. This grief is then totally overturned by full participation in joyful celebrations of their deliverance. So these two aspects of the narrative's design are linked in the character of Esther. She participates in the *status quo* to effect change for her people who are God's people, in a way that points to the story's theological meaning.

iii. Style

The story of Esther is written from the narrator's point of view. Clues to the characteristics of the narrator's representation are gained from looking more closely at stylistic features, such as the characterization, language, pace and mood of the story.[27] It is clear that the narrator adds his own insight to the Esther story: he inter-prets the characters' thoughts and feelings and, of course, designs the story and adopts language that supports his perspective.

a. Characterization

One of the striking features of characterization in Esther is that the characters emerge not through their own words but through the narrator's words. There is very little direct speech in the book (in clear contrast to the book of Ruth, for example). So Mordecai has only one short speech (4:13–14), despite his important role in the story. The reader does not eavesdrop on conversations so there is a distance between the reader and the story. The narrator seems more concerned with action than with characterization, conveying information rather than provoking empathy. So it has been suggested that it is only Esther who develops in any sense as a char-acter. The other characters are static. They remain what they always

---

27. See Long (1999), who argues that we need to consider details such as perspective, order, duration, summary, ellipsis, story-time, stretch and pause, as well as the functions of syntax, linguistic semantics and pragmatics, if text analysis is to be fruitful.

were and they are typecast. There is similarity with the traditional typecasting of the wicked and the righteous in the wisdom literature. So, for example, we see Haman as wicked and full of folly and misdirected aggression; Mordecai, on the other hand, is righteous and wise, and his anger is channelled in the right direction and in the right way.[28] In particular, righteous people react with a sense of proportion to the circumstances facing them, whereas the wicked have no sense of proportion.[29] It is sometimes argued that flat characters best suit the comic genre of the story, for it makes the characters themselves unreal and suggests that they should not be taken too seriously. While this may help to understand the priority of the narrator – action rather than characters – in some senses the story of Esther is the story of its characters, and therefore what we discover about them should not be overlooked.

We gain most of our insight about Xerxes (Ahasuerus) from the descriptions of how his court operates. He emerges as a bumbling and self-indulgent man, motivated by his own sensual appetites. His court is regulated and bureaucratic, but escapism and merriment dominate his horizons. The operation of the court centres on the king's whim, making for an uncertain and unpredictable environment. Most of all, the king is capricious and malleable, without personal conviction.[30] His exposure in the first two chapters of the book sets the scene: the Jewish people are dangerously vulnerable. Xerxes is the only character who is around for the

28. This reading of the characterization of Haman and Mordecai is not, however, as clear-cut as it might seem. It could be argued that the whole crisis is brought about by Mordecai's stubbornness (Esth. 3:2) rather than his wisdom and righteous anger.

29. Bechtel (2002: 7–10) suggests that proportion is an important theological theme in the book, which starts with the disproportionate feasting in the Persian court (ch. 1) and ends with the celebrations of chapter 9, which are completely in proportion to the salvation the Jews have experienced.

30. As Firth (1997: 19–20) says, 'a dangerous autocrat and someone to be manipulated by those about him … something of a buffoon who is scarcely able to rule'.

duration of the story: the constant is that just as he was only apparently in charge at the start, so also at the end, though now Esther and Mordecai have assumed control rather than his courtiers.

Haman is not bumbling, he is evil through and through. When he is introduced, his honour is mentioned first (3:1), but any optimism about this man quickly disappears through Mordecai's response to him (3:2) and then by the unveiling of his irrational anger and plans (3:5–6). Insight into Haman's inner thoughts exposes all that he is, and like the exposure of Xerxes, this adds tension and irony to the story. The narrator does not allow his readers any doubt: Haman is doomed from the outset and we are to enjoy witnessing his downfall. The narrator aligns himself in opposition to Haman, allowing the heroine Esther to denounce him in a dramatic declaration before the king (7:6), after which Esther's term is adopted and Haman is labelled 'the enemy' (8:1; 9:24). Chapter 6, often seen as pivotal in the story, portrays a man with a reeling and tortured mind subject to the irrational forces of his own wickedness. In this chapter he is transparently devious. Although Haman himself is irrational, his downfall is completely rational – he cannot be protected from himself, and his death on his own gallows (ch. 7) is both ironic and inevitable.

In contrast, Mordecai is protected by some degree of mystery. We are not told the motivation for his actions, nor are we given clues about his emotional state (for example, we are left to guess why he refuses to honour Haman, 3:2). The narrator protects Mordecai from too much scrutiny, and in this way preserves his heroic status. Mordecai's characterization doesn't really develop, although his leadership qualities are universally recognized at the end. Instead, he remains a constant example of personal strength, integrity and conviction. He is a man of neither whim nor irrationality, and acts as a counterbalance to the instability depicted through the characters of Xerxes and Haman. It is Mordecai's actions that distinguish him from those around him: he is an exceptional man of his times and even Haman cannot ignore him (5:13). He is also 'of the Jewish people' and it is left to Zeresh to voice this reality and its significance to her husband (6:13).

Uniquely in this book, the characterization of Esther has movement and development. Esther begins as a pawn in a volatile game. She is subject to other people's expectations and whims, and things happen to her rather than through her. However, even in the early stages of the narrative there are hints that there is more to Esther than passivity and outward beauty (2:7), as she 'wins' favour (2:9, 15). By the middle of the story it is clear that Esther is intelligent, courageous and persuasive (chs 4 and 5), and she now starts to give the orders (4:15) and dictate the actions and schedules of both the king and Haman (ch. 5). By the end of the story Esther's rise as the story's heroine is complete: she assumes control (ch. 8); and she is now the one who writes a decree 'with full authority' (9:29). She devises a strategy and executes it, and her real strength of character emerges with the story's outcome. This character development enables the reader to identify with Esther. She is human – not always strong. At a decisive moment she resolves to act (4:15) and thereby turns around her life and the lives of others. In this sense she is the inspirational character of the story – one to whom the reader can aspire.

The other characters, Vashti, Zeresh, the court officials, the Jews as a whole, play supportive roles as agents moving the plot along or providing contrasts and pairings with the other characters. As a group, these human characters are subject to providential events: the coincidences of the story in which they take part point to the limitations of their power. These coincidences, and the unlikely outcome of the story, force the reader to think about where power ultimately lies: what is God's part in the story?

b. Language

One of the striking features of the book is the lack of religious language. There is no mention at all of God or his commands or his relationship to his people. This, along with the excesses in the language, makes Esther unique among the biblical books. This uniqueness is perhaps explicable in terms of the ironic comedy within the book and the carnival occasion with which the story became associated.

The clearest example of exaggeration occurs in association with the numbers that appear in the story: 127 provinces, a 180-day plus 7 days party/banquet, 12 months of beauty treatments,

10,000 talents of silver and a stake measuring 50 cubits. The effect is to make the details ridiculous. Lists of unpronounceable names also appear (1:10; 1:14; 9:7–10), which slows the pace for the reader, leaving the impression that these names are deliberately ludicrous.

Dense repetition litters the text. The writer uses repetition as a form of emphasis and sometimes as a way of underlining the folly of the character involved. Chapter 6 exemplifies this. In Haman's speech (vv. 7–9) the repetition highlights the devious contriving nature of the story's villain, but then the repetition is continued as the king takes over, and ironically everything Haman planned for himself happens to Mordecai. In Chapter 5 the king's own weakness is depicted by his repeated offer to Esther, 'What is your petition … what is your request? Even up to half the kingdom, it will be granted' (vv. 3 and 6). Esther wisely repeats Ahasuerus' words back to him (vv. 7–8).

The hyperbolic style is furthered by the use of synonyms. On numerous occasions, the narrator says the same thing more than once by providing alternative words of similar or identical meaning. So on hearing the king's edict, the Jews mourn with 'weeping and wailing' and in 'sackcloth and ashes' (4:3), and Esther describes the decree as selling her people 'for destruction and slaughter and annihilation' (7:4). Complementing this prolific use of synonyms are the dyadic expressions where the same word is used twice in one phrase to emphasize totality. In addition to the prolific use of *kol* (every), we have word repetition, so 'every province' is literally 'every province and province' (4:3), 'every city' literally 'every city and city' (8:17), 'each man' literally 'man and a man' (1:8) and 'each province' literally 'province and a province' (8:9).

This style introduces sound patterns and alliteration to the text, just as the lists of unpronounceable names do. While such features are not unique to Esther, their prolific use in this narrative text results in a unique piece of literature.[31]

---

31. See e.g. Brenner (1995: 73), who concludes that taken together these features are a message as well as a medium, for by them a tale becomes political satire.

c. Mood

By the mood and tone of the text, folly and wickedness are ridiculed. That ridicule becomes even more effective because it is coupled with a sense of fun. Despite its subject matter there is lightness to the story – it is a story the Jews would love to tell and celebrate; it is made easy to bear. The mood is ironic and dramatic and is established through contrasts and reversals. In decisive moments, elaborate schemes are undone by unplanned coincidences. The result is a mood of optimism and expectation for its readers, as the downfall of the story's villain begins to pan out. Not surprisingly the most ironic and dramatic moments in the story centre on Haman and his demise (for example, 5:12; 6:11; 7:8–10). In his demise is the elevation of Esther and Mordecai, and the optimism is realized.

d. Pace

In the main the tempo is fast, the exception being the elaborate descriptions of the court as the narrative opens, carefully setting the scene for the story. Decisions are made with great speed: there is little time for careful reflection when Vashti is deposed (1:10–22), when the decree about the Jews is issued (3:8–15), or when Haman gets whisked off to attend Esther's banquet (6:14). The movement of characters is emphasized at the start and end of each scene, allowing the story to gather pace – there are no easy places to stop when reading this story. In addition, the reader has access to only the gist of speeches and edicts, for the gist is enough to allow the story to sweep on.

e. Tension

Despite the fast pace, some literary devices are used in the story to cause suspense and create tension. Esther's insistence on a further banquet (5:8) holds up the events of the story temporarily. Then we reach chapter 6, which interrupts the story-line and prepares the way for the reversals to begin. Suspense is also created by the passive voice that dominates the early scenes, giving the impression that no one is in control and anything could happen. This said, suspense only works at a basic level – the irony ensures that the reader still expects good to conquer evil.

These features of literary style (or as Brueggemann [2002: 360] prefers, 'the artistic processes') illustrate the writer's concern to present his story in the way that best suits his intentions. It seems that the writer wanted his story to be told and re-told but also enjoyed and re-enjoyed, and his literary choices were part of his commitment to his readers.

f. Unity

Advocating the unity of the book of Esther seems a viable position, despite the concerns that have been raised over the origins of chapters 9 and 10.[32] Certainly a sense of unity is maintained throughout the Hebrew text by the theological motifs (feast and reversal), which give the book its structural balance. However, there does seem to be a change of style at least at 9:20, where the rhetorical is replaced by a less flamboyant, direct style. The final form of the Hebrew text may indeed reflect different sources and interests, but it also stands in its final form as a coherent text with a historical core in which, possibly, religious, festival and pictorial dimensions have been successfully integrated. Whether these dimensions reflect the work of a single writer to suit his own purposes, or many writers to suit their own purposes, is debatable, but the text is clearly intelligible and meaningful in the Hebrew form in which it is preserved.

Because of the unique combination of literary issues and stylistic features in Esther, it is inevitable that discussions about the book's meaning and purpose will always be related to assessments of its

---

32. R. Kossmann (1999) suggests that only chapters 1–7 are the work of one author, relying on different sources but writing a non-Jewish 'Pre-Esther' text with later redactors adding the remaining chapters. Contrast Fox (1991: 115), who argues for one author who chooses to follow his sources closely in chapters 1–7, expands on them (ch. 8) and then builds on them (chs 9 and 10). Houk (2003) has examined the syllable-word patterns in Esther and has concluded, with Clines (1984b), that Esther 1:1 – 9:19 in its present form emerged from three different writers. However, Houk's method of statistical analysis has been criticized by O'Keefe (2005: 409–437), who concludes that more work is necessary on natural variation and genre of texts before Houk's conclusions are accepted.

literary character. The way the story is told, as well as the story itself, testifies to its purpose, and the design of the text is both the instrument of its meaning and the instruction itself.

6. Textual issues

The textual history of Esther is a complex issue. There are many different forms of Esther in different languages, which reminds us of the complicated history and development of the scriptural text. Most scholars now agree that there are at least four important witnesses to the story of Esther: the Hebrew Masoretic Text and three Greek versions.[33] But behind these texts themselves is envisaged a variety of early text forms (both written and oral). The textual history is complicated by decisions made by the Christian church over many years, whereby various versions based upon diverse texts have either been accepted or refused acceptance into the canon.

i. The Hebrew Masoretic Text

The Hebrew version of Esther is the shortest of the extant witnesses to its story. Additionally, the earliest manuscripts of the MT date from the eleventh century AD (a long time after the earliest Greek manuscripts), so we don't actually possess an 'original' Hebrew text or anything like it. However, the Hebrew manuscripts are uniform in their presentation of the consonantal text of Esther. It wasn't until the time of Jerome (fourth century AD) that the Christian church became focused on uncovering the original Hebrew text of the OT canon. Until this point, the church accepted Greek versions as the texts they relied on. Jerome's preference for translating and interpreting the Hebrew text of Esther was reaffirmed when the Vulgate became the Bible of the Western church. Additional sections of Esther without Hebrew manuscript support were relegated to an appendix. During the Reformation, there was a resurgence of interest in the Hebrew language, and it was the Hebrew text that was the basis for Luther's own translation of the Old Testament (completed in 1534). Even

---

33. See Dorothy, 1997: 13.

though there are uncertainties about its own sources,[34] no one has doubted the importance of the Hebrew text as a witness to Esther's story – it is, after all, the text followed by the Syriac and Aramaic versions – but the Greek texts too cannot be ignored.

ii. The Septuagint (LXX) or 'B-text'

This standard Greek translation of the OT was produced in the third to second centuries BC and is preserved totally in fourth-century AD manuscripts. Origen was certain that this translation was based on the original Hebrew text of the OT. Despite Jerome's dissatisfaction with the text (he designated the additions of the Septuagint as deutero-canonical), it was afforded great importance by Augustine, who believed that because the Septuagint was the first Bible of the Christian church it should be universally accepted. It seems certain that the Septuagint was the Bible that the church used once the Christian message was taken outside Palestine by Paul and others. A Greek translation was necessary for non-Hebrew-speaking Christian converts, including Jews of the Diaspora. One of the implications, therefore, is that the Septuagint may reflect a Hebrew text earlier than the MT, which would have had equal status with the current Hebrew text as sacred Scripture.

The Septuagint of Esther has six main units of text, which are not reflected in the MT; some appear to be Semitic in origin, others Greek. These have become known as the six 'Additions' and are referred to by the letters A–F.[35] Jerome's removal of the Additions from his Vulgate text had the unfortunate effect of isolating the six texts from their place within the Esther story, so their context became unclear. The author of these Additions is unknown, though some of them are traditionally associated with Lysimachus who translated the text of Esther into Greek in about 114 BC. The Additions add new dimensions to the Esther story by their focus on

---

34. See, for example, Clines (1984b: 114), who discusses whether the MT text relied on at least two sources (the Esther and the Mordecai stories) and if chs. 1–8 were the original book, as ch. 8 brings the story to a successful conclusion. He labels this shortened version 'the proto-masoretic text'.

35. See Appendix, p. 156.

God and prayer, and by changing the story's mood, movement and details in places. In particular, the name of God is introduced, Purim is not emphasized and the characterization of Esther is different. The resulting story is judged to be in line with the emphasis in Ezra/Nehemiah and Daniel, and whatever the purpose of the Additions, this similarity probably aided the canonical acceptance of Esther. The Septuagint certainly shows us how Greek-speaking Jews of the pre-Christian era read and understood the story of Esther, and therefore its witness to early Jewish interpretation cannot be disregarded. The Greek Additions are still an integral part of the OT canon for Roman Catholic and Eastern Orthodox churches.

iii. The 'A-text' ('L' or Lucianic)
Four Greek manuscripts (dating from the tenth–thirteenth centuries) preserve a text of Esther, again much longer than the Hebrew version. Originally, the text was thought to belong to the Lucianic recension (originating with Lucian of Antioch, d. 311/312), but this is now doubtful. It is possible that this text relies on the LXX, but this is not certain.[36] We might surmise that a proto-A text existed, without the Additions, which itself may have been based on a non-Masoretic Hebrew text. Such an explanation accounts for its connections with the Hebrew text, as well as the fact that it does not duplicate it. Although the history of the development of the A-Text is uncertain, it does bear witness to a form of the Esther story that was accepted among Greek speakers in the tenth–thirteenth centuries. Indeed Dorothy (1997) suggests that the A-text contains the earliest known form of the core tradition and therefore demands greater attention than it has received. He argues that the A-text adapts the Esther story to make it more palatable to a less-Hellenized community based in Palestine. He suggests that this explains the apparent Jewishness of the text when compared with the other known versions of the story. Indeed, in the A-text Esther makes no attempt to hide her Jewishness, God's covenant with Abraham is repeatedly mentioned, and God's acts of

36. See Tov (1982), who suggests that the A-text was based on LXX, but then corrected to another Semitic text.

deliverance are emphasized. The independent nature of the text is quite evident from these few examples of its uniqueness.[37]

iv. The version of Josephus

This version of the Esther story in Josephus' *Antiquities* (II.184–296) is important because of its early date (first century AD). It has generally been portrayed as a paraphrase of the Hebrew version, but we should allow the possibility that Josephus' version bears witness to a text other than the MT. It is possible that the version relies on a 'proto-MT' text or, of course, an independent tradition altogether. Josephus' story is considerably longer than the MT and gives evidence of the text and interpretation of Esther in Josephus' own era and setting. Josephus' narrative adds its own frame narrative along with some details not found in other texts. However, because it does not contain Mordecai's dream and its interpretation, and only has a précis of Esther's prayer, its text is shorter than the Septuagint and A-text. Josephus offers a little less irony than the other forms of Esther. This may be explained in light of its character as historical narrative and its religious point – God watches over his people. Unfortunately, detailed research on the relationship of Josephus' text to the other versions of Esther remains unfinished.

Recent studies of the textual history of Esther have encouraged us to appreciate more fully the independent nature of these textual witnesses. In particular, it is less acceptable simply to read the Greek texts as 'supplements', merely providing additions to a superior Hebrew text. If we accept that all four main texts are indeed separate books of Esther, or separate witnesses to the Esther story (evidencing different eras of textual transmission within the communities from which they come), then each witness should be allowed to inform our understanding of this story at least to some degree.[38] The Protestant church needs to consider the implications

---

37. For further discussion, see Fox (1991a) and Clines (1984b).
38. Dorothy (1997: 360) concludes that the Greek versions need to be considered as entire coherent texts, if their value is to be truly appreciated and if their witness is to 'live on'.

of this, but it at least re-emphasizes the role of the faith community at the centre of canonical decisions from the outset. We should remember that canonical discussions concentrated on listing canonical books rather than highlighting the particular textual version that was acceptable. For this reason, the various texts that bear witness to the Esther story have a vital role to play in informing our appreciation of the history of interpretation arising from diverse faith communities over the centuries.

7. Theology and purpose

Perhaps the most outstanding theological feature of the Hebrew text of Esther is that it makes no mention of God at all. For some, this means that it lacks theological value altogether, but its place within the canon denies the possibility of such a stark conclusion. Furthermore, fundamental to Jewish and Christian theology is the view that where God's people are to be found, God is actively present, and certainly Jewish presence is central to the Esther story. So we need to grapple with why God's name is not mentioned, while holding onto a theological perspective that prefers to talk about the 'hidden' God in the text rather than the 'absent' God.

Early attempts to understand the omission of the divine name in Esther concentrated on the nature and content of the text of Esther and its use by the Jewish community. There was the suggestion that the party atmosphere of the Purim festival was an unsuitable context for God's name to be mentioned. This seems an unsatisfactory explanation, especially as liturgies of this festival include words of blessing which use God's name both before and after the reading of the Esther text. The non-mention of God's name has also been explained by looking at the book's genre (e.g. the absence of God's name is to be expected in a book designed as a Persian chronicle[39]). This line of argument also has circularity as its weakness, especially when we consider that assigning the book to this literary form has already taken into account its apparently non-religious character. Further, it has been argued that Esther is primarily a story of non-

---

39. Gordis, 1981: 359–388.

religious nationalism, and the inappropriate behaviour of God's people in the story itself demands that God is hidden. Some of these perspectives pay more attention to the content of the story than to the author's design or purpose. It is certainly feasible that the story does not mention God's name because the author assumes God's presence rather than mentions it. Equally, it could be maintained that the author is concerned with leading readers to their own faith-reading of the text, rather than imposing such a reading.

Here I believe we move closer to the author's intentions. We have already seen that the author adopted a style and genre that encourage the story to be told and re-told, enjoyed and celebrated. The style causes the reader to feel involved in the story, somehow participating in its journey, but with attention on the story's movement and outcome rather than on individual details. We have noticed the testimonial value of the text – the theme of salvation and reversal is a testimony to preservation despite the odds – and this is surely the significance of the story within the Jewish cycle of festivals. Accounts of salvation are always faith-creating and faith-confirming, and somehow Esther conforms to this norm without the necessity to identify that it is God's hand at work. In other words, the text serves as an invitation. It is as if the author says, 'I am inviting you to hear this story and to respond to it with faith.' This journey to faith requires pondering the events, searching for God within the plot, and choosing to see his active presence. So the story 'veils' God's presence rather than hides it, teasing the reader to look beyond the veil to the greater reality that can be uncovered through searching.[40] The story requires a response to the mystery of the veiled presence of God. This response is faith-creating and faith-building, for it is a personal and individual response rather than a second-hand one, built only on the author's own interpretation of the story. But what sort of faith is encouraged by the story? Certainly such faith conforms to the basic tenets of Christian theology, incorporating at different levels some key theological assertions:[41]

40. For this idea of 'veil', see Fox, 1990: 135–147.
41. In the notes that follow, only occasional reference is made to individual verses in the text. It is possible to proof-text these theological

i. God is working his purpose out

The providence of God is hinted at through the use of coincidence and surprise within the text. Coincidences occur which are left unexplained but which dictate the outcome of the story as it moves towards the moment of reversal and resulting salvation. So, for example, Esther is in the right place at the right time when Vashti is deposed (2:8) and when Haman's evil plans come to light (4:14b). When the king cannot sleep and asks for his historical records to be read, they happen to fall open at the page that highlighted Mordecai's role as the one who foiled an evil plot against the king (6:1–2). As the king considers what to do, it just so happens that Haman is standing outside (6:5), and the resulting honour to Mordecai fuels Haman's anger. The frequency of such coincidences promotes the legitimacy of a theological reading of the text in which the providence of God is at work. Furthermore, because the path of this story does not conform to human expectations and there are elements of surprise that defy human explanation and reason, such a reading seems to be encouraged. In Esther the ultimate surprise is that 'the tables were turned' (9:1). This phrase interprets the great moment of reversal in the story, and although the text says that the Jews now get the upper hand, no subject is identified as the over-turner of tables. In Christian theology, God is often identified as the one who brings reversal. He turns darkness into light, mourning into rejoicing, defeat into salvation and death into life. In the lives of God's people, such reversals defy human explanation and reason, whether they happen in the lives of individuals (like Joseph, Daniel, Hannah, Saul and Jesus himself), or to groups of his people (from wilderness to Promised Land, from exile to return, from the place of crucifixion to the place of resurrection). They serve as examples of the dramatic intervention of God bringing about his purposes through his people's preservation and ultimately by his Son's gift of salvation to the world.

---

observations, but I believe that the theological meaning of the story lies in the whole rather than in its independent details, and I have attempted to respect the author's own theological perspective.

A reading of the text that allows a providential focus makes sense of the place occupied by this text in the history and life of the Jewish people. At this point in their history, the Jews clung onto the hope that God's providential hand guarded their lives, despite the external forces to which they were subject. To read the story of Esther without this perspective makes the story more, not less, incredulous. As Purim festivals were celebrated in each year of their perilous history, the story of Esther served as a reminder that even in their darkest days God's people could trust in the providential care of a covenant God who had promised to be with them for ever.

ii. God is presently active in the world

It seems undeniable that the world-view of the Esther story includes the belief that God is actively present in the world. This is the hope that makes sense of the story's 'lightness'. There is optimism from the outset that the Jewish people will survive, and in this story that belief is not linked to the return to Jerusalem, to the adherence to cultic practices, or to the emergence of an expected Messianic figure. In Esther the active presence of God goes beyond these boundaries of geographical and religious expectations. God is actively present in the world of Esther and Mordecai. They too, in a foreign land subject to secular rulers and régimes, can become instruments of God's active presence. As Israel's history unfolded, the story was relevant not only to the original community of its setting but to every generation since. It demonstrated in practice the universal and eternal operational presence of the covenant God who lives up to his name: Yahweh, the one who is eternally active and present in the world.[42]

---

42. The meaning of the name 'Yahweh' is often discussed in relation to Exodus 3:14. Durham (1987: 39) suggests that 'I am who I am' means 'I am the Is-ing one', i.e. 'I am the one who always is and always acts.' This explanation is remarkably apt in the context in Exodus where Moses visibly sees the presence and activity of God as he leads his people in the wilderness. The name 'I am' comes to Moses with the promise of God's presence (3:12) and his activity (vv. 16 and 17 – where the emphasis lies on God's imminent work of sovereign intervention).

iii. God works with human behaviour and responses to him

Esther's story illustrates that God can work with or without human co-operation. While it is necessary for Esther to make the conscious decision to take up the challenge to work for God's people (4:16), it is not necessary for Haman to actively pursue God's purposes in order for God's people to be saved. Anderson (1950: 40) puts it this way: 'even the most disreputable characters and flagrant violators of his will are bent into the service of his ultimate purpose.' In other words, God's purpose may include human agents, but its success does not depend on who those agents are or what they do. Esther herself is not flawless in the story: hiding her identity contradicts Jewish law; the process of becoming Xerxes' queen is unsavoury; instituting laws that are vicious appears morally indefensible. But God works with these human responses as his sovereign will for his people emerges.

iv. God protects and saves his people

The story's meaning is clearly tied up with the perspective that Israel occupies a protected and privileged place within God's purposes.[43] This is what gives the story its timeless quality. The Jews would continuously remind themselves of the events in the book of Esther because they are eternally illustrative of a theo-logical reality: God saves his people. The story dramatizes theology, and this dramatic presentation is worthy of the miraculous nature of the salvific act it records.

Theologically the question remains: does the intrinsic value of the text lie in its message about the Jews or its message about their Saviour? In other words, is the story primarily about God or his people? Of course, for the covenant community there was no such dichotomy: God is defined by his people, and they by him, just like

---

A number of parallels exist between Esther and Mordecai and Moses (see comments on 4:14) – not least in terms of their own participation in God's purposes, as instruments of his presence in his world.

43. This view is hinted at by Mordecai (4:13–14), and even Zeresh's words (6:13) show a limited awareness of God's protective activity in the history of his people.

a shepherd is known by his flock, and the flock by him (Ezek. 34). So the people of the holy God are called to be a holy people (Deut. 7:6), and the significance and direction of history is tied up with God's relationship to his people and theirs to him. When God intervenes in their lives, his nature as well as their status are revealed.[44]

These observations are certainly compatible with the view that the purpose of the story's place in the canon relates to its faith-creating role. It is because God can be trusted as Saviour that his people can exercise faith that is saving. For its original readers, for Jewish people and for Christian readers, Esther becomes part of their *Heilsgeschichte* (salvation history), the reason for their faith. It promotes trust in a God who saves all people who turn to him in faith. This life of faith and trust is the real promised rest for which his people longed.[45]

v. God's people can celebrate

The book of Esther does not hold back: when good things happen, even miraculous things, God's people will rightly celebrate (8:16–17). The institution of the festival of Purim provides an opportunity for God's people to celebrate regularly (9:18–22). It reminds them that evil was defeated, and such a victory parades laughter and enjoyment as suitable emotional responses. There is little solemnity in the Purim festival, but lots of hilarity and celebration. The evil context in which victory came is subsidiary and that evil itself is reversed by the generosity that marks the festival (9:22). Within the OT, gratitude to God and trust and confidence in him leads to deep joy that pervades worship. Frequently such

---

44. So, e.g. with the statement 'God planned it for good' (Gen. 50:19–20), God's intervening action and his nature are defined, as well as the status and fortunes of Joseph in God's plans.

45. The Promised Land is intimately tied up with the idea of rest in the OT. But for God's people as their history progressed, the homeland sometimes became a distant memory and the hope of rest becomes associated with the life of faith. So Psalm 62:1[2] 'my soul finds rest in God alone'.

trust and joy emerge from dire circumstances, as the Psalms often show us.[46] It is important to note the commendation of celebration in the Esther text. Throughout history, God's people are called to exercise the faith to rejoice in God in all circumstances, but certainly to respond to acts of deliverance with celebration and praise.

vi. God calls his people to faith

The Purim festival is a reminder that Jewish history results in a faith that needs to be practised. There is no point knowing history but not living in the light of that history. Faith for the 'here and now' makes sense of the 'there and then'. The purpose of divine activity meeting human behaviour correlates to the faith that is produced. Esther is arguably a role model of faith and piety, but her story is more than that: it promotes faith and piety. It is a story that encourages every reader to understand 'what is going on' in 'what is going on', and to respond accordingly with a life of faith and devotion. Every situation, whether or not God's presence and power can be seen or felt, is an opportunity for a divine encounter, a place to experience God's intervention, and therefore is a situation worth experiencing.

Perhaps the author of Esther is determined that God's presence remains 'veiled' in the text because this is the very point. Perhaps the author's own faith journey has been one where the presence of God has never been particularly evident. Is the author encouraging us to be people of faith even when our most common experience is at best that God is hidden? Is he in fact saying that this is what life and faith are normally like? Visions and revelations might come and go (as the apocalyptic literature suggests), but the veiled presence of God is a constant that may not be seen and felt but will always sustain his people in good, bad and ugly times. This is the precious truth that Esther's story celebrates.

---

46. See e.g. Psalm 35, where in a section about grave injustice the Psalmist declares that his soul rejoices in the Lord and takes delight in God's salvation (v. 9). See also Psalm 108 (a combination of Pss. 57 and 60), which is a prayer for help filled with words of celebration and trust.

The author of Esther is calling readers to 'do theology' – to reflect on God's nature and his seen or unseen role in history. But 'doing theology' also includes responding to the implications of such a quest, and this responsive task will even today require individual and corporate faith as a heart response to God's self-revelation.

ANALYSIS

1. INTRODUCTION: THE REIGN OF XERXES (AHASUERUS) (Esther 1:1–9)

A. The stage is set: 'in the days of Xerxes …' (1:1–2)
B. The royal banquets (1:3–9)
    i. Xerxes' banquet for his officials (1:3–4)
    ii. Xerxes' banquet for the people of Susa (1:5–8)
    iii. Vashti's banquet for the women of Xerxes' palace (1:9)

2. ESTHER BECOMES QUEEN (Esther 1:10 – 2:20)

A. The demise of Vashti: 'on the seventh day' (1:10 – 2:4)
    i. Vashti is summoned by Xerxes (1:10–11)
    ii. Vashti refuses to obey the summons (1:12)
    iii. Xerxes takes advice from his wise men (1:13–15)
    iv. Memucan's proposal (1:16–20)
    v. Xerxes accepts Memucan's advice (1:21–22)
    vi. Xerxes accepts the advice of his young men (2:1–4)

B. The emergence of Esther: 'now there was ... a Jew' (2:5–20)
    i. Esther's family history (2:5–7)
    ii. Esther's rise to favour (2:8–9)
    iii. Esther's secret (2:10-11)
    iv. Explanation of the selection process (2:12–14)
    v. Esther is selected as queen (2:15–17)
    vi. Queen Esther's banquet (2:18)
    vii. Queen Esther's loyalty to Mordecai (2:19–20)

3. THE PLOT AGAINST XERXES: 'in those days' (Esther 2:21–23)

A. The plot is discovered by Mordecai (2:21)
B. The plot is foiled (2:22–23)

4. HAMAN'S PLOT AGAINST THE JEWISH EXILES: 'after these things . . .' (Esther 3:1–15)

A. Haman's power (3:1–11)
    i. Haman's rise to power (3:1–2)
    ii. Haman's anger against Mordecai (3:3–5)
    iii. Haman plots the destruction of all the Jews (3:6-9)
    iv. Haman is now in charge (3:10–11)
B. The edict of genocide (3:12–15)
    i. The edict is written (3:12)
    ii. The edict is distributed (3:13–15)

5. MORDECAI AND ESTHER RESPOND TO HAMAN'S PLOT: 'when Mordecai learned ...' (Esther 4:1 – 5:8)

A. Esther discovers Haman's intentions (4:1–9)
    i. Mordecai weeps in sackcloth (4:1–4)
    ii. Esther investigates through Hathach (4:5–9)
B. Mordecai enlists Esther's help (4:10–17)
    i. Esther's unenviable position (4:10–11)
    ii. Mordecai challenges Esther (4:12–14)
    iii. Esther accepts her role (4:15–17)
C. Esther hosts a banquet (5:1–8)

    i. Esther issues the invitation (5:1–5)
   ii. The banquet is held and a further invitation is issued
       (5:5–8)

6. HAMAN'S PLOT AGAINST MORDECAI: 'filled with rage against Mordecai' (Esther 5:9–14)

A. Haman's emotional turmoil (5:9–13)
B. Haman accepts his wife's (and friends') advice to hang
    Mordecai (5:14)

7. XERXES HONOURS MORDECAI: 'the man the king delights to honour' (Esther 6:1–11)

A. Mordecai's loyalty is remembered (6:1–3)
B. Xerxes takes advice from Haman (6:4–9)
C. Mordecai is publicly honoured (6:10–11)

8. PARTIAL SUCCESS: THE DEATH OF HAMAN (Esther 6:12 – 7:10)

A. Haman's demise: 'you will surely fall …' (6:12 – 7:6)
    i. Zeresh and advisers predict Haman's downfall (6:12–14)
   ii. Esther's second banquet takes place (7:1–2)
  iii. Esther exposes Haman and his plot (7:3–6)
B. Haman's death (7:7–10)
    i. Xerxes' anger is aroused (7:7–8)
   ii. Haman is put to death (7:9–10)

9. FULL SUCCESS: THE JEWISH PEOPLE ARE SAVED (Esther 8:1 – 9:16)

A. Mordecai and Esther find favour before Xerxes (8:1–4)
B. The issue of overturning Haman's edict is addressed
   (8:5–14)
    i. Esther asks for a new edict (8:5–6)
   ii. Xerxes hands the matter over to Esther and Mordecai
       (8:7–8)

iii. Mordecai oversees the writing of a new edict (8:9–10)

iv. The new edict is distributed (8:10–14)

C. The Jews' mourning is replaced by joy (8:15–17)

i. Mordecai's honour is complete (8:15)

ii. The Jews' gladness is complete (8:16–17)

D. The enemies of the Jews are destroyed (9:1–16)

i. 'now the tables were turned' (9:1–5)

ii. The extent of the Jewish victory in Susa (9:6–12a)

iii. Esther's further request on behalf of the Jews in Susa (9:12b–13)

iv. Esther's request is granted (9:14–15)

v. The extent of the Jewish victory in the provinces (9:16)

10. THE JEWS CELEBRATE THEIR VICTORY (Esther 9:17–32)

A. Spontaneous days of feasting (9:17–19)

B. Mordecai himself confirms the festival (9:20–22)

C. The festival of Purim is established (9:23–32)

i. A summary of the festival's historical roots (9:23–26a)

ii. A summary of the commitment of the Jews to this festival (9:26b–28)

iii. Esther confirms the festival (9:29–32)

11. CONCLUSION: MORDECAI'S HONOUR: 'he worked for the good of his people' (Esther 10:1–3)

COMMENTARY

1. INTRODUCTION: THE REIGN OF XERXES (AHASUERUS) (Esther 1:1–9)

Context

This opening section of the story of Esther serves two purposes. First, it provides a historical setting; secondly, it introduces the reader to the world that setting represents.

A. The stage is set: 'in the days of Xerxes …' (1:1–2)

The first two verses place the story within a historical framework, without which it does not make sense. It is because *this* king reigns that the plot can develop. The vulnerability of the Jewish people is assumed as soon as Xerxes' status and sovereignty are mentioned – his controlling power versus their vulnerability is a central theme in this story.

Comment

1. The narrative begins, *This is what happened during the time of* (NIV), which seems a predictable phrase to start a new narrative. However,

its varied translation in other versions (cf. RSV, NRSV, NKJV) hints at
the rarity of this compound. Within the OT, historical narratives
usually use 'this is what happened', whereas prophetic writings opt
for the second half of the compound 'during/in the days of'. These
opening words may alert the reader to the quasi-historical character
of the story (or folklore-like, see Berlin [2001: 5), comparing the
compound to 'Once upon a time, in the days of the great and
glorious Ahasuerus …'). Alternatively, the compound may serve to
connect the story with preceding historical narrative (cf. Gen. 14:1;
Isa. 7:1; Ruth 1:1)[1]. Thus the compound does not necessarily imply
the story's historicity, but neither does it rule it out.

Xerxes is the Greek form of an old Persian name meaning 'he
rules over men/heroes'. The Hebrew text has *'ăḥašwērōš* (cf.
Ahasuerus in some modern versions, e.g. NKJV, NRSV and RSV). The
preference for Xerxes (NIV) has emerged because it is the recognized name for the Persian king who was the son of Darius I, to
whom the Greek historian Herodotus bears witness. Xerxes (b. 518
BC) ruled between 485 and 465 BC and appears on only one other
occasion in the OT (Ezra 4:6), when he opposed the re-building of
the temple. Xerxes was certainly a powerful oppressor but his rule
ended in humiliating defeat at the hands of the Greeks. His desire
for excessive glory led him to make military errors when all the
numerical advantages had been his. Xerxes' reign is a suitable setting
for the story, but it is possible that the writer did not intend to bring
a historical king to mind (which may account for the humorous
sound of the Hebrew name and the Greek alternative rendition,
Arta-xerxes), but created a world for the story that bore similarities
to a historical world. However, the overlap between the author's
presentation of this king, and the presentation of Xerxes by
Herodotus, is too great to dispense with lightly.

127 provinces stretching from India to Cush describes the extent of
Xerxes' sovereignty. The author could have described Xerxes' reign
by mentioning the larger administrative districts (satrapies) that
made up his empire (Herodotus says there were initially only about
twenty of these, though perhaps thirty-one over time). Instead, he

---

1. See GK, para.111.2g, p. 327.

refers to smaller areas *(mĕdînâ)*, probably associated with individual cities (see Neh. 7:6; Ezra 2:1; Dan. 2:49), and chooses the largest possible way of numbering them, hence exceeding even Daniel's recognition of 120 provinces (see Dan. 6:1). *India to Cush* designates the geographical (rather than the administrative) extent of Xerxes' reign. Cush (English 'Ethiopia', now north Sudan) denotes the province in the south-west corner of the empire. India (now south Pakistan) was added to the empire by Darius and lies in the south-east corner.

2. The king's royal residence is in *the citadel of Susa* (NIV, NRSV). Although sometimes translated as 'capital' (RSV) or simply 'city' (LXX), perhaps 'palace' (NKJV) in the sense of the palace and its environs, or 'citadel', are preferable. This term, borrowed from Akkadian, was particularly used for the high ground at the centre of the city of Susa where Darius built the Persian palace. This is supported by the use of the word in 1:5 (description of the palace gardens) and the fact that edicts are issued from the citadel (3:15; 8:14–15). This fortified area, a favourite winter residence for the Persian kings, was where Xerxes took refuge after his defeat at the hands of the Greeks (480 BC).

The city of *Susa* was the pre-eminent city among four capital cities used by the Persian rulers. Situated in Elam (south-west Iran), about 240 kilometres north of the Persian Gulf, it had the advantage of being situated in a fertile plain with plentiful rivers.

Meaning

Susa sums up the success and pleasure this king enjoyed. The citadel at Susa was a physical representation of Xerxes' physical comfort and security, and the success and glory of his reign. The overview is in place: Xerxes is reigning happily. Now the writer's view narrows to a particular time in his reign.

B. The royal banquets (1:3–9)

Context

This descriptive section is punctuated by the formula *he/the king/the queen gave a banquet* (vv. 3, 5, 9). The repeated phrase adds movement to the narrative that is otherwise excessively detailed. There is no dialogue, no explanation of the banquets' purpose, and the language seems hyperbolic in purpose. It is significant that the theme of feasting features at the start and end of the book of Esther, as well as at the centre of the story (chs. 5–7).

Comment

i. Xerxes' banquet for his officials (1:3–4)

3. This first feast is excessive in terms of its participants (v. 3) and its duration (v. 4). It is held *in the third year of his* (Xerxes') *reign* (i.e. in 483 or 482 BC, after Xerxes' campaigns in Egypt and Babylon). Irony may be intended here because Esther's first readers knew that this period of carefree rule was abruptly ended by Xerxes' unsuccessful campaigns against the Greeks. This banquet was possibly part of the warm-up for Xerxes' war council that planned the attack against the Greeks. Certainly the author schedules this banquet so that its timing is both historically viable and ironically significant.

The exact meaning of *nobles, officials, military leaders, princes* and *nobles of provinces* is debatable, though they are probably people groups honoured by appointment rather than by birthright. Even the divisions within this list are not straightforward, because the conjunction is used in a seemingly random manner. The list as a whole clarifies that this banquet was for the great and the mighty, for those who upheld the structures that supported Xerxes' rule.

Additional note: Persia and Media

The Medes and the Persians are two related people groups, both Indo-European Iranians, who migrated south from Russia into the Iranian plateau. In the early years after migration the Medes were a decentralized group, but by the early seventh century they established a capital city and a state. They experienced a level of success in 612 BC, joining with the Chaldeans to take the Assyrian capital city, Nineveh, but under Cyrus II (559–530 BC), who had a Median mother and a Persian father, the Persians eventually absorbed the Medes and their independence was lost. Consequently Esther 1:3 refers to Persia first as the controlling force.

4. *180 days* may be the length of this first banquet or the length of the display of the king's wealth. The writer emphasizes the ridiculously lengthy nature of the king's self-glorifying celebrations (it would be impossible for all these important officials to be relieved of their duties for half a year!).

ii. Xerxes' banquet for the people of Susa (1:5–8)

The purpose of this banquet is not explicitly identified, though its attendees and its duration may inform our conjecture. It may have marked Xerxes' wedding to Vashti, as everyone in the service of the palace was invited to join the celebrations which lasted seven days (cf. the bridal week for Jacob and Leah, Gen. 29:27). The quality of decorations (v. 6), the free flow of wine (vv. 7–8) and the demand for Vashti's appearance (v. 10ff.) are consistent with a wedding banquet.

5. The setting is *in the enclosed garden of the king's palace*. Excavations of Persian palaces suggest that the citadels housed the palace buildings surrounded by gardens decorated with murals and water features. The gardens also contained pavilions supported by columns serving as large outdoor banqueting halls. This area appears to be the location of the banquet (cf. Bush 1996: 347).

The invitation is extended to *all the people who were in the citadel of Susa* (i.e. including people not among the select company invited to the first feast, but restricted to those who served the king in the citadel). It is likely that a residential area existed within the citadel of Susa, so there were plenty of people to invite.

6. The guests are treated to overwhelmingly lavish surroundings (v. 6) and provisions (v. 7). It is hardly possible to string together a more luxurious description than that in verse 6. The writer seems overwhelmed by the scene he describes and piles on the images of luxury . The syntax is unusual and creates the effect of poetic exclamation. The royal colours, white and purple, bring majestic tones. The intended impact is visual rather than verbal, and the use of rare words supplements the exotic picture that is created. Although the descriptions have hyperbolic effect, even Greek writers and Jewish tradition describe Persian palaces in luxurious terms.

7. The *goblets of gold* demonstrate Xerxes' wealth. The Persians generally used glass or metal vessels but brought out the gold

vessels on special royal occasions (cf. Dan. 5:2). The vessels here are individually designed indicating Xerxes' flamboyant style. The wine was *abundant* and literally 'according to the king's hand' (NIV *in keeping with the king's liberality)* (cf. 1 Kgs 10:13, which uses the same phrase to describe Solomon's generosity to the Queen of Sheba when he wanted to impress her!).

8. Even the amount of wine to be drunk was not restricted, for the king issued a *command* (*dāt* not *tôrâ*) that there was to be no 'law' (restriction). This hints at Xerxes' lack of moral fibre: his 'law' permits a lawless free-for-all. However, it is possible that this verse implies that Xerxes gave up his right to dictate the duration of wine drinking – normally it would be expected that guests drank wine for as long as the king did. But in this opening scene it seems more likely that the intention is to highlight the indulgence of the banquet.

iii. Vashti's banquet for the women of Xerxes' palace (1:9)

This third banquet for women receives little comment. The author starts with the most magnificent and lengthy banquet, moves to a shorter banquet, and then arrives at this understated event.

Queen Vashti enters the story as host of the banquet. Even though Persian men and women often enjoyed banquets together, royal queens were excluded from social occasions where drunkenness and licentious behaviour featured. It seems that Vashti's banquet was an indoor affair (*in the royal palace*, better 'royal house or hall') in contrast to the outdoor setting of Xerxes' banquet.

The name *Vashti* sounds like the Persian for 'beautiful woman', possibly indicating that this is the Persian name for the queen, referred to by Herodotus by her Greek name Amestris. Herodotus tells us that Amestris was queen when Xerxes was involved in the campaign against the Greeks, and he identifies her as the mother of Artaxerxes.

Meaning

The reader has been introduced to the Persian world typified by Xerxes and his palace at Susa. The descriptions exaggerate the grandeur and wealth of Xerxes who places his honour on ostentatious display. Xerxes' honour is challenged immediately by the first real incident of the story that follows.

Additional note: The Palace of Susa

French excavators found extensive remains of the palace in Susa, built by Darius in 490 BC and subsequently occupied by Xerxes. The palace 'was decorated with friezes of coloured tiles, showing divine animals and floral patterns. In particular, a handsome frieze of gaily coloured tiles in relief representing in life-size a parade if the Great King's bodyguard of Bowmen, called the Immortals, may be mentioned. A figure from this frieze … shows a bowman wearing long Elamite dress, holding a spear' (Barnett 1966: 78). The ornate detail, the bright colours and the very size of this frieze support the description of the palace in Esther 1. A detailed account of the history and the physical appearance of the palace of Susa, based on archaeological evidence, is provided by Yamauchi (1990: 279–303). Of particular note is the claim that the palace of Susa was decorated more ornately than any other Persian palace and that its structure was highly complex. Inscriptions also indicate that materials (gold, cedar timber, precious stones, silver, ebony) were brought from all over the realm to decorate the palace (e.g. stone columns came from a village in Elam; stone-cutters were Ionians and Sardians; Babylonians baked bricks; and the Medes and Egyptians provided decoration for the walls). In this way, the palace was 'owned' by the realm as a whole and it was due to such labours that Xerxes inherited his ornate palace complex.

2. ESTHER BECOMES QUEEN
(Esther 1:10 – 2:20)

Context

Now the historical and political scene has been set, attention turns to a necessary prelude to the main story. This prelude is an example of how the Persian court operates, and thus perhaps confirms the reader's suspicions about Xerxes' modus operandi. The narrative comes to life as the action begins and conversations are recorded, although it is not until Vashti is deposed and Esther is enthroned that the main story can emerge.

With the incidents that are unveiled in this prelude, Xerxes' world is disrupted by a female presence that threatens his power. The operations of Xerxes' court are ridiculed through the incident of Vashti's demise, but when Esther replaces Vashti, another banquet is held to celebrate Xerxes' honour.

A. The demise of Vashti: 'on the seventh day' (1:10 – 2:4)

This first real incident highlights Xerxes' weaknesses. First Vashti does not comply with his wishes and then Xerxes shows his inability to make decisions. The incident explains the rather unlikely outcome that a young Jewish orphan girl becomes queen in Persia, and adds tension to Esther's story because her vulner-ability as queen is at least equal to Vashti's. Vashti vanishes from the text as quickly as she appeared. She gives a banquet (v. 9), refuses to come for the king (v. 12), and then is talked about rather than talked to. Her quick demise, and the lack of interest in her motives or her future, suggest that the author is concerned with the political chaos her experiences expose, rather than the justice of her individual fortunes.

Comment

i. Vashti is summoned by Xerxes (1:10–11)

10. Xerxes' summons to Vashti was issued *on the seventh day*, the climax of the banquet. The banquets were opportunities for the king to honour himself, and the appearance of Vashti was part of that (note the word *display* appears in vv. 4 and 11). The phrase *in high spirits from wine* (NIV) can imply both cheerfulness ('merry': NKJV, RSV, NRSV) and drunkenness. The Hebrew literally reads 'when the heart of the king was *good* with wine'. A 'good heart' on account of wine is associated with negative outcomes (see e.g. 1 Sam. 25:36 and 2 Sam. 13:28). Perhaps Xerxes' state of mind explains Vashti's non-compliance and hints at why Xerxes needed to involve his seven eunuchs: he was not capable of fetching her himself.

The names of the eunuchs (or officers, though castration is probable for their role) have some connection with known Persian names, but the forms are twisted, making this list (like others in this book) seem ludicrous. This, along with the use of the number seven again, suggests that the author is concerned with the effect of the record rather than the record of history. Seven eunuchs to bring in one queen seems unnecessarily pompous, and the pronun-ciation of each name draws attention to the farcical nature of this episode (cf. the next list of seven in v. 14).

11. Xerxes instructs Vashti to appear *wearing her royal crown* (prob-ably some form of ornate turban). This may imply that she was to be otherwise naked (as rabbinic interpreters over the years have suggested). It seems that Xerxes intended to present Vashti as his property – her crown is a royal one and her significance relates to him. The throne (v. 2), wine (v. 7), palace (v. 9), decree and position (v. 19) are all 'royal' possessions (cf. Laniak 1998: 46). It is the king's presumption that Vashti exists only to serve his purposes that makes her non-compliance intolerable.

ii. Vashti refuses to obey the summons (1:12)

Vashti *refuses to come*. As Fox aptly puts it, 'Vashti said no. This is the entirety of her direct portrayal' (1991: 164). Nonetheless, Vashti plays an important role. Her refusal to come sees her replaced by Esther who comes boldly and is accepted by Xerxes even when she is not invited (Esth. 5). Esther works in the same arena as Vashti and from this early point in the story the reader knows that men like Xerxes *burn with anger* when wilful women confront them. Vashti violates Xerxes' honour, whereas Esther uses his honour to bring down Haman (Esth. 7). Xerxes' responses to both violations of honour are not surprising: 'In honor based societies shaming constitutes a grave offense which regularly produces the most extreme responses' (Laniak 1998: 56).

iii. Xerxes takes advice from his wise men, adding tension to the narrative (1:13–15)

These verses discuss *what must be done to Queen Vashti?* (v. 15). Apart from the short statement that she is never again to be allowed before the king (v. 19), they don't elaborate on Vashti's punishment.

13. Confronted by disobedience and his own rage, Xerxes seeks the advice of *wise men who understood the times*, possibly a category of the *experts in matters of law and justice*. Herodotus (*Histories* 3:31, cf. Ezra 7:14) suggests that the Persian kings had appointed judges who decided lawsuits and interpreted laws and customs. It seems that 'law', joined with 'judgment'(*dîn*) – making a nice alliterative doublet – is used to refer to a range of legal processes. (NB NRSV attempts to emend *times* to 'laws', but this is unnecessary. It is generally agreed that the *men who understood the times* were not astrologers or lawyers but all-round experts.)

14. The list here sounds similar to the list in verse 10: seven eunuchs to fetch the queen, now seven advisers to deal with her. These men with *special access to the king* were the nearest thing to friends and peers that the king had. It is startling that Xerxes' question is devoid of emotion, driven only by procedural interests. Xerxes gives the responsibility for determining procedure to his advisers. This early demonstration of Xerxes' weak leadership and lack of authority allows for Haman's abuse of his delegated power and Esther's ability to turn around Xerxes' will.

iv. Memucan's proposal (1:16–20)

The king's advisers, led by Memucan, 'fabricate a crisis out of nothing and come up with a proposal that throws the spotlight on their own embarrassment' (Fox 1991b: 168). The issue about Vashti is turned into a policy to protect themselves and the honour they think they deserve as husbands. Even Xerxes' interests appear to be of secondary concern to the interests of his nobles. Vashti is even credited with wide-ranging influence over all the wives of the nobility (vv. 17–18).

One of the longest speeches in Esther is recorded in verses 16–20. Memucan puts the Vashti incident in a wide-ranging context by asserting that Vashti has *done wrong ... against all the nobles and the people of all the provinces.* Is it possible that Memucan, aware of the king's personal embarrassment, deliberately removes the spotlight from the king? Alternatively, it may be that Memucan's personal insecurity drives him to be concerned with the general issue of women rebelling against their husbands. There is clearly some irony attached to Memucan's speech (note the quantum leaps in logic and the repeated use of 'all', allowing for no exceptions to the behaviour and consequences outlined).

16. Memucan's primary concern is that husbands will be despised (i.e. scorned or dishonoured, cf. v. 18) by their wives. This contrasts with 'respect' (NKJV, RSV, NRSV 'honour') at the end of Memucan's speech (v. 20). The Vashti incident, like all incidents in this court, is assessed in terms of the honour it brings. Although Memucan is careful not to say directly that Vashti has brought dishonour on Xerxes, the implication is clearly there.

18. Memucan suggests that *this very day* Vashti's behaviour will

be imitated and will bring *disrespect and discord* (better perhaps
'despising and anger') to the nobles' households 'according to suffi-
ciency' (NIV, NRSV 'no end of'; NKJV 'too much'; RSV 'in plenty').
Xerxes is saved from criticism: no one mentions that if women are
to imitate Vashti, men first have to imitate Xerxes!

19. So a decree is required to make an example of Vashti.
Memucan advises that this should be *written in the laws of Persia
and Media, which cannot be repealed,* which would of course propa-
gate Vashti's infamy. 'Cannot be repealed' means 'cannot pass
away or become obsolete', and although the tension in this narrative (see also Dan. 6:9, 13, 16) relies on this idea, it does not find
support in other Persian or Greek sources. This means the phrase
could be hyperbolic rather than literal – 'make a decision and stick
to it!'

Vashti is stripped of her royal title and is banned from the king's
presence. Her punishment fits her crime, but ironically Vashti is
given permission to do exactly what she wants to do – stay away
from the king. Some Jewish interpreters suggest that this is a eu-
phemism for Vashti's execution for we hear nothing else of her.
However, Vashti's fate is not the focus of the story: her non-
mention has more to do with the author's purpose than necessarily
implying her execution. Vashti's punishment allows Esther's
appearance to be anticipated through an initial assessment of her
character as *someone else who is better than she* (cf. 1 Sam. 15:28).
Although this phrase is delightfully ambiguous, for Memucan this
is about submission to the king's whim (it doesn't figure in the
criteria for the new queen's selection, ch. 2).

20. The irony is blatant: to stop women imitating Vashti, an edict
must be proclaimed so that there will be widespread honour for
husbands everywhere. Hidden in some English translations is an
interjection that praises the king's realm (see NIV 'vast'; cf. NKJV 'for
it is great' and NRSV 'vast as it is'). The phrase could be translated
'throughout all his realm – how magnificent it is – and all the
women …' This example of court flattery suits the context, for,
by ending his speech with flattery, Memucan ensures that his advice
seems good (v. 21)!

Meaning
Memucan's speech demonstrates a movement from Xerxes' procedural concerns to Memucan's personal fears. His anxiety becomes Xerxes' anxiety as Memucan capitalizes on the Persian obsession with honour.

v. Xerxes accepts Memucan's advice (1:21–22)

Context
This narrative summary confirms the execution of Memucan's plan. Verse 22 explains the purpose of the edict as giving men authority in their own homes. That such an edict issues from a king who has not been able to induce obedience when it really mattered to him is plainly ironic. The tone adopted is instructive and indicative of what is to come.

Comment
   21–22. The Hebrew text compresses a variety of ideas together in a hyperbolic style, so an exact translation is difficult and is possibly less important than the impression and pace it is meant to convey. The Persian communication system is set into motion to communicate the edict, which is translated into different scripts and languages. These details are entirely consistent with what we know from Herodotus about communication and multi-lingual culture in the Persian Empire. There is verbosity and spiralling bureaucracy here. The decree was to achieve universal distribution, and no excuse would be permitted for not understanding it.
   The end of verse 22, providing the purpose of the edict, reads literally 'every man should be ruler in his own home and speak according to the language of his people'. Although the meaning is ambiguous, note that Nehemiah 13:24–25 addresses the issue that the Jews' language was no longer prevalent in Jewish men's households. Here the point is that men should assert authority in their homes, and using their own language was one way of doing this.

Meaning
Chapter 1 ends with a description of the Persian court in bureaucratic operation, in contrast to the court in self-honouring

merriment at the start of the chapter. Both perspectives form part of the backdrop onto which the story is painted.

vi. Xerxes accepts the advice of his young men (2:1–4)

Context

These verses conclude the prelude before Esther and Mordecai enter the story. All the luxury of Xerxes' court takes second place to the proliferation of women now, but both emphases serve as statements about Xerxes' priorities. Vashti's place is legally vacant so Xerxes consults his young male servants, who advise him about how to replace her.

Comment

1. The chapter begins with the familiar 'after these things', which indicates that some unspecified time has passed since the end of chapter 1. Verse 16 clarifies that Esther is taken to the royal residence in the seventh year of Xerxes' reign (ch. 1 took place in his third year [1:3]). During the intervening time, Xerxes may have been more concerned with the campaign against the Greeks than with his personal circumstances. Xerxes *remembered Vashti* (possibly an expression of regret) but the blame still lies with *what she had done*. Xerxes does not recall here what caused the incident in the first place.

2. Xerxes' attendants (see also 3:3) notice his melancholy mood and offer him some rather obvious advice. In effect they say 'cheer up, Xerxes, find the most beautiful woman in your realm and make her queen instead! No time for regrets!' (cf. the advice of David's attendants, 1 Kgs 1:2–4). Rather than *virgins* (NIV) the word *bĕtûlôt* means 'women of marriageable age', although in Persian society it would be assumed that such women would be virgins in the technical sense of the word.

3. Again the plans go into overdrive as the advisers suggest the appointment of *commissioners in every province* to bring together the beautiful girls *into the harem at the citadel of Susa* (or, more literally, 'to the house of the women in the citadel of Susa', cf. NKJV). This suggests that there was a particular part of the royal residence reserved for women of the king's harem. Hegai was officer in charge of preparing the women for their service to the king. He organizes *beauty treatments* or more exactly 'rubbings' (from a Hebrew verb meaning 'to polish or rub or scrape'). This may indicate massage or skin exfoliation, but, given the length of time permitted for these treatments, the inclusive and non-specific *beauty treatments* (NIV) is appropriate.

4. Herodotus tells us that Persian queens were normally selected from one of seven noble families in Persia, but no such concern features here. The young woman who pleases the king most will *be queen instead of Vashti*. There are no restrictions on this king's wishes and the stage is prepared for the emergence of Esther. The king once again accepts and assents to his attendants' advice without questioning it.

Meaning

Vashti's demise is preparatory, but also essential, to the story's development. She serves two key purposes: to demonstrate Xerxes' weaknesses and to make Esther's selection as queen plausible. She might have a third role – does she alert Xerxes to his own misjudgment? There are certainly no recorded attempts by Xerxes to show off Esther for his own gratification in the way he wanted to use Vashti. Perhaps, therefore, Vashti saves Esther, the story's heroine, from inappropriate treatment at the hands of a volatile and rigid king.

Additional note: Feminist interpretations of Esther I

It is not surprising that this story has received feminist analysis, focusing on the characters of Vashti and Esther. Traditional interpretations have discussed Vashti as an example of a rebellious wife, while Esther has been honoured as a submissive wife. In the light of such readings, which barely show any regard for contextual and literary context, feminist interpreters understandably want to reclaim Vashti and re-examine Esther.

Feminist writers have highlighted the positive elements of Vashti's non-submission. They have emphasized that her non-compliance shows strength of character which challenges the male behaviour of a patriarchal society that was structured around power and abuse in political and personal relationships. In a similar way, Esther is interpreted as an example of feminine intelligence that wields its own power, even when it encounters male

domination. Such assertions give some consideration to the historical and social context of the story:

> There is a violent demonstration of the ruling class against women, which
> makes Esther a book with a theme of sexism.[1]

Other writers emphasize that Esther is a book that complies with
the expectations of patriarchy:

> The Hebrew text is written from a male perspective. It imposes a norm
> on women. It appears to have been written by men for men, and for
> women.[2]

In other words, sexism is not a theme in the book, because norms
are not challenged, but only assumed. Certainly there are no explicit
evaluations of Persian societal norms, although the satire in the
narrative may be implicit comment. However, most of the satire is
saved for Xerxes as an individual egotist rather than as a representative of unacceptable patriarchy. So for some feminist interpreters,
Esther remains a story based on unacceptable male presuppositions.

The danger with feminist interpretations is that main themes can
be ignored by virtue of a special focus. It is important that the first
chapter of Esther should be understood as providing the setting
for the story. The chapter does not necessarily highlight the book's
theme; it sets the scene for that theme to emerge. In the end, this
chapter is more about Xerxes' court than it is about either Vashti
or Esther, for it is the way Xerxes exercises his reign that is ultimately the threat to the Jewish people and the focus of the story.

For this reason it is prudent not to contrast Vashti and Esther as
both traditional and feminist interpreters have sometimes done. In
this epic about Jewish survival against the odds, both women take
a stand that sets in motion a string of events so unlikely that God's
providence is assumed. It is the Persian court that makes both their
contributions remarkable. As Bush states:

---

1. Bea Wyler in Brenner 1995: 132.
2. De Troyer in Brenner 1995: 70.

> Vashti's refusal to be shown off like a common concubine before the tipsy hoi polloi of the citadel of Susa reveals a sense of decorum and self-respect that places her outside of the mocking characterisation that the narrator has given the rest of the royal court.[3]

Vashti's refusal to obey the king is a comment on Xerxes rather than on the patriarchy of the society he represents. As such, it weakens Xerxes' honour and power, which the story in turn capitalizes on through Esther's own role. So like Vashti,

> Esther like virtually all biblical heroines, finds her place in Scripture not as one who has effectively changed – or even challenged – the social order. Rather she has contributed, through bravery and intelligence, to the divine purposes for Israel.[4]

In this sense Vashti and Esther do not champion the feminist cause. They champion the purposes of God that allow Gentile and Jew, the privileged and the orphan, women and men, to contribute to the outworking of his salvation for his people. The crisis in the story centres not on male/female power but on Persian power versus Jewish vulnerability. When times are particularly critical, it seems that God chooses to work in unexpected ways by reversing roles and redistributing effective power. The author did not intend to bring a feminist perspective but a theological one, and this original intention must be allowed to instruct our reading of the text today.

B. The emergence of Esther: 'now there was ... a Jew' (2:5–20)

Context
The prelude is over, the main characters are introduced and the main story begins. This is marked by a change of word order and tone (lit. 'A man of the Jews there was in the citadel of Susa', v. 5). This section explains Esther's arrival in the palace and her selec-

---

3. Bush 1996: 354.
4. Laniak 1998: 164.

tion as queen. There are some repetitive elements, but otherwise the text is matter-of-fact, contrasting with the elaborate descriptions in chapter 1. Esther's low status and powerlessness contrast with the honour and power of Persia. She represents Jewish vulnerability as her story becomes intertwined with, and illustrative of, their story. Hope emerges as vulnerable Esther receives grace and favour and finally is honoured by a banquet of her own (v. 18). Her rise to queen consort anticipates the possibility that her people's story can also be transformed.

i. Esther's family history (2:5–7)
Although these verses interrupt the flow of the story (v. 8 follows on from v. 4), they are an important interjection. Esther is introduced through Mordecai, anticipating their joint importance in the ensuing story.

Comment
5. With an economy of words, verses 5 and 6 introduce Mordecai and his family line. Mordecai is described as 'a man of the Jews'. In Hebrew narratives it is common for the controlling aspect of a new character's identity to be emphasized by being placed at the start of the sentence, as here, hinting at the character's role in the story (cf. Job 1:1; Gen. 24:16; 37:2; Judg. 4:4; Dan. 1:4; 1 Sam. 16:12).

The name Mordecai (in the MT, his second designation) is similar to the name of the Babylonian god 'Marduk' and a common Babylonian name 'Marduka'. Mordecai is probably the Hebrew equivalent of this common name. An inscription at Persepolis, another royal city, mentions a Marduka as one of Xerxes' officials, adding some historical credibility to the author's choice of main male character (Yamauchi 1990: 235).

The summary genealogy of Mordecai, 'son of Jair, son of Shimei, son of Kish, a Benjamite' (NB this word order is retained in RSV, NRSV and NKJV) helps us to set this story in the wider context of Jewish history. It associates Mordecai with King Saul, for Shimei was a member of Saul's clan (see 2 Sam. 16:5–8); Kish was Saul's father, and Saul belonged to the tribe of Benjamin. This connection between Saul and Mordecai is significant, because Haman is

introduced as an Agagite (Esth. 3:1) whom Mordecai eventually
overcomes, whereas Saul lost his throne because he chose to spare
the Amalekite King Agag (1 Sam. 15). So Mordecai's loyalty to the
Jewish people supersedes that of King Saul, and Mordecai becomes
representative of God's redemptive presence among his people.
As Levenson (1997: 57) usefully puts it, 'Mordecai rises on the very
point on which Saul fell.'

6. This verse seems to place Mordecai among the people exiled
by Nebuchadnezzar in 597 , along with Jeconiah. This would make
Mordecai about 120 years old when Xerxes started to rule (cf. NRSV
that adds 'Kish' to the start of v. 6, understanding the relative
pronoun to refer to Mordecai's great-grandfather). Perhaps the
writer's priorities here lie outside producing a precise history. By
this reference he stresses that Mordecai and Esther are from the
upper classes of the exiled community (note the common people
were exiled in 587 BC and the root *glh* [exile] appears four times in
v. 6 alone). This is important to the story, because although
Mordecai and Esther have access to the king's courtyard (2:11; 3:3),
they remain vulnerable as powerless people, even if honoured by
their own people as faithful in exile.

7. Esther is introduced in dependent relationship to Mordecai:
she is his uncle's daughter and he has adopted (Hebrew 'taken')
her into his home as his own daughter. These details establish two
things: first, Esther is expected to behave in submissive obedience
to Mordecai; second, there is nothing untoward about her position in his house. The LXX suggests that Esther was taken as
Mordecai's wife rather than as a daughter. Whether this reflects
traditional adoption procedures or whether it attempts to remove
any hint of improper behaviour is unclear. However, it makes the
story more complicated, because if Esther is Mordecai's wife, then
she actually commits adultery with Xerxes. There is nothing in the
Hebrew text to suggest that Mordecai is anything other than a
caring cousin.

Esther's Hebrew name is 'Hadasseh', probably derived from a
root meaning 'myrtle'. (Some rabbinic traditions refer to Deut.
31:18 where the root *str* ['to conceal'] occurs, producing a consonantal text comparable to what we have here. This fits with Esther's
decision to 'conceal' her identity.) By mentioning her Hebrew name

first, the author emphasizes that although Esther inhabits two worlds, her primary identity is Jewish. Esther is the Hebrew transliteration of a Persian name, probably derived from the word meaning 'star'. Again, it was probably both a common name and the name of a Babylonian goddess 'Ishtar' (cf. comments on Mordecai above). The first description of Esther is as 'lovely in form and features', and it is her beauty that is decisive in her selection and operation as queen. However, her tragic beginnings receive double mention in this verse, perhaps to invoke sympathy.

ii. Esther's rise to favour (2:8–9)

8. The story resumes with the carrying out of Xerxes' order. No mention is made of Esther or Mordecai's response to it, just that Esther was passively 'taken' (producing a parallel with the enforced exile, v. 6). Now Esther is a member of the exiled community but is also exiled from her family home. Her personal fortunes echo the fortunes of the Jews as a whole; she is just one of many young women rounded up for Xerxes' benefit.

9. Esther soon 'pleases' and 'lifts up favour [kindness]' from Hegai (see NKJV 'she obtained kindness of him'). Hegai's attention is drawn to Esther and he cares for her just as Mordecai has done. But Esther also works for this favour – she draws it out of Hegai (cf. also vv. 15 and 17 where she 'lifts up' favour from everyone including Xerxes himself). The word translated 'favour' is the covenant term *ḥesed* (usually used to describe God's loving kindness and mercy towards his people). Esther wins advantages: she gets beauty treatments, food parcels and maids straightaway. The emphasis is on the speed of obtaining these gifts rather than the fact that these were exceptional presents. Beauty treatments have already been anticipated in verse 3, and food parcels (Hebrew *mānôt* 'food delicacies'), possibly intended to fatten up or improve the complexion of consumers, were also offered to Daniel (Dan. 1:8–16). Esther is also promoted (lit. 'transferred') to *the best place in the harem*.

So Esther is poised for success, but the tension is increased again by a further interjection (cf. also vv. 5–7 above).

iii. Esther's secret (2:10–11)

Whether explanatory, secondary or a literary device to create suspense, these verses contain information that is important to the development of the story (so important that it is repeated in v. 20).

The main plot of the story (Haman's intent to destroy the Jews) relies on Esther's Jewish identity being secret. There is no attempt to explain why Mordecai did not want Esther to disclose her relationship to him or to the Jewish people. We may surmise that Mordecai was concerned about prejudice against Esther, based on either her family or her nationality, or both. What is clear is that Mordecai remains influential in Esther's life and she respects his wishes.

While the concealing of a secret adds a pending sense of danger to the next scene, the reader is assured that Mordecai has not abandoned Esther to her Persian surroundings. He remains close at hand.

iv. Explanation of the selection process (2:12–14)

These verses intrude into the story of Esther's rise by explaining the details of the selection process to which all the gathered women were subjected. The author protects Esther – she is not directly mentioned while the degrading process, with all its extravagance and sexual overtones, is described. The author's tone may be ironic (especially as the length of the beauty treatments reflects the length of banquets at the start of ch. 1) but there is no criticism of these procedures, just a plain statement that this is how the system operated.

12. The verb meaning 'to go into/to enter' occurs three times in these verses and it is loaded with sexual overtones (cf. Ruth 4:13 and 2 Sam. 11.4). The preparation for one night with the king is extravagant in length and luxury. Whether the women literally bathed in oil and perfumes or whether these provisions were burned on incense burners is unclear,[5] but obviously no expense was spared. The length of time for each treatment is

5. Archaeologists have found incense burners. See Yamauchi, 1990: 253–254. See also references to spices and perfume in the context of lovemaking that litter the Song of Solomon (e.g. 1:3; 1:12–13; 4:6, 10, 14 etc., and also Prov. 7:17–18; Ruth 3:3).

prescribed (*dat*) – even these practicalities are governed by law.

13. Although it seems that the young women had no choice about the length and nature of their preparation, when their turn arrived and they were moved from the harem to the king's private quarters, they had some say about how they presented themselves. *Whatever the girl asked for* may have included items of clothing or jewellery or aphrodisiac foods (some of the descriptions of preparations for love-making in Song of Songs provide possible insight here). The writer does not supply the details but leaves that to the readers' imagination. The provision of 'anything' contrasts with Esther's modest request (v. 15), and is a feature of Esther's queenship – she is often given the chance to ask for anything (cf. 5:3, 6; 7:2; 9:12).

14. The Hebrew word *šēnî* (either 'second' or 'again') may indicate that the harem of Shaashgaz was a second separate harem, or that the women simply returned to the harem after their night with the king, but now Hegai was no longer responsible for them.

Note that after their night with the king the women were presumably consigned to a lifetime of waiting to see if the king would call them again. It is clear that this selection process was as much about sexual performance as it was about natural or enhanced beauty. The end of the verse suggests a rather depressing fate for each woman, which adds tension to Esther's reappearance in the narrative.

v. Esther is selected as queen (2:15–17)

Attention is turned from the description of the process to Esther's emergence within it. Somehow, despite the seediness of the process, she emerges as modest and wise, winning favour from all sorts of people (Hegai, v. 9; everyone, v. 15; the king, v. 17). The language becomes formal, emphasizing the critical nature of this moment. Esther is introduced again (this time by her father's name, v. 15) and a detailed time schedule is announced (v. 16).

15. Esther chooses to submit to Hegai's advice. The inference is not that Esther rejects all the trappings offered to her, but that she is prepared to go with Hegai's recommendations. Despite this passive acquiescence, the writer observes that Esther has a role in her own destiny, 'winning' favour from everyone (cf. comments on v. 9 above).

16. Esther *is taken* to the king four years after Vashti was removed (cf. 1:3) in the month of Tebeth. This is the Babylonian name equivalent to December or January (see Introduction, Origin and date, pp. 21–22). The intervening four years may indicate a delay before the selection process began (see p. 81 above) or that it took Esther some time to emerge in this process.

17. The king responds to Esther most positively of all. She wins his grace and favour and more significantly (so at the start of the sentence) 'the king loved Esther more than all the other women' (NRSV; see also NKJV, RSV). The verb *'hb* has wide-ranging meaning in the OT (ranging from deep emotion to passing fancy), coupled with *favour and approval*, as here it seems that the king was deeply impressed by Esther at a number of different levels. Although the norm was for women to be sent back to Shaashgaz to await further summons, Xerxes makes Esther *queen instead of Vashti* straightaway. Esther has assumed Vashti's crown and position, and in doing so, she, like her predecessor, is both honoured and at risk.

vi. Queen Esther's banquet (2:18)

Whereas Vashti gave her own banquet, the king gives a banquet for Esther to which *all his nobles and officials* are invited (cf. Vashti's banquet for the women) and the wider community also benefits.

The exact nature of the benefits is unclear. The Hebrew word used (*hanāḥâ*) means 'remission', 'suspension' or 'rest' (hence NKJV 'a release'), so translations tend to preserve one of the two possible meanings, 'remission of taxes' (RSV, cf. 1 Macc. 10:25–35) or 'holiday' (NIV, NRSV). Other unspecified *gifts* are also distributed (possibly deliberately vague, implying that all sorts of relief and gifts were granted). By such an emphasis Esther's arrival on the Persian scene is immediately perceived as good news by her people.

vii. Queen Esther's loyalty to Mordecai (2:19–20)

These verses re-emphasize the points made in verses 10–11. They recall Mordecai's devotion to Esther and Esther's secret. Both these facts are crucial to the story.

Verse 19 brings reality to the euphoria of the previous verse. It reminds the reader that Esther operates in an environment that uses and abuses women who can be gathered at a whim. This is balanced by the reminder that Mordecai is still close at hand for Esther: he sits *at the king's gate*. This is significant because, first, it allows Mordecai to hear the plot against the king (vv. 21–23), but secondly, it confirms that Mordecai had some official role. The king's gate was a large building where the palace administration was housed and where justice was dispensed (Yamauchi 1990: 298–300). It appears that Mordecai assumed some responsibility in this process.

Meaning

Esther 2:5–20 allows Esther to emerge and finally become queen. Passive verbs are mainly used in relation to Esther, suggesting that she is not responsible for the situation in which she finds herself. Instead, she makes the best of her precarious environment and is received favourably by those in whose hands she is placed. At the start and at the end of the section, Esther's Jewish heritage and her relationship to Mordecai are stressed. The two main characters operate in a Persian context but the emphasis is plain: this story is about Jews and Jewish history, not Persians and Persian history. It's about Jewish faith and its survival in a pagan world.

3. THE PLOT AGAINST XERXES:
'in those days' (Esther 2:21–23)

Context

The importance of this incident is sometimes overlooked on account of its brevity and style, but it presents new elements that are critical to the story's development. It takes place some time between Esther's selection as queen (the seventh year of Xerxes, 2:16–17) and Haman's plot against the Jews (the twelfth year of Xerxes, 3:7). It is reported in curtailed Hebrew sentences that mark it out from the surrounding text. In form the report here may reflect what was written in the king's record (v. 23). There are no embellishments, no exaggerations, no literary finesse, but instead plain statements of fact.

The incident creates suspense, precedes the appearance of the story's crisis, and anticipates and intertwines subsequent themes. Prior to Haman's introduction (3:1), it portrays Esther and Mordecai as loyal servants of Xerxes. This positive portrayal stays with the reader as Mordecai's conflict with Haman is exposed.

Comment

A. The plot is discovered by Mordecai (2:21)

Bigthana (cf. Bigtha, 1:10) and Teresh are simply introduced as officers (lit. 'eunuchs', cf. 1:10) of the king and 'door-keepers' or 'guards of the threshold' – probably meaning they were the last line of defence for the king (like secret police or informers). There is no characterization as such for these men. Their crime is literally that 'they sought to send out a hand against King Ahasuerus', an idiom for an assassination attempt. Certainly such attempts against the king's life were not unusual and often find a place in historical records. In fact, although Xerxes survived this attempt on his life, he was killed in a palace plot in 465 BC, which involved the assassin being taken into the king's private quarters at night-time by the king's chamberlain (see Yamauchi 1990: 239).

B. The plot is foiled (2:22–23)

Mordecai was in the right place simply to overhear the plot being construed, but verse 22 states that the plot 'came to the knowledge of' (or 'was revealed to') Mordecai, allowing the possibility that he was told about it. His response is to tell Queen Esther who in turn tells Xerxes. Later on, this pattern of communication is repeated with regard to Haman's plot (see chs. 4 and 7). Here Esther and Mordecai are recognized as trusted sources of information for Xerxes, who has a justified level of paranoia about his personal security. It is surprising in the light of their close working relationship that the king doesn't uncover Esther's family secret. But maybe this too is planned for ironic effect: this administration, so full of bureaucratic safeguards, cannot see what is blatantly obvious.

On investigation the plot was 'searched out' and 'found out' (NIV *investigated and found to be true*). No explanations are given but the result is plainly stated: 'both of them were impaled on a tree' (NIV *the two officials were hanged on a gallows*). This does not refer to actual execution (contrast the Greek renditions of this account which use the word for crucifixion here), but to the public disgrace of dead bodies of shamed people being hung for all to see (cf. Deut. 21:22;

Josh. 8:29 and 1 Sam. 31:10). This foreshadows Haman's shaming (ch. 7), where the extraordinary height of the gallows exaggerates the public display of his shame. These verses produce an interplay of the themes of shame and honour: Xerxes should have been honoured by his eunuchs but wasn't; Esther is honoured as Queen; Mordecai acts honourably but isn't honoured; and the eunuchs are totally shamed. This is in preparation for Haman's abrupt entry as honoured and elevated (3:1), but for no apparent reason.[1]

The final comment emphasizes that the incident was written down *in the presence of the king*, and therefore presumably with his consent and approval. This practice is referred to again in 10:2, where the records of the king are mentioned as testifying to Mordecai's greatness. These records played a role in perpetuating the memory of people and their actions.

Meaning
This short episode completes the description of the circumstances in which the crisis of the story is set. It is a likely event, given what we know about Persian court affairs, and is told with the simplicity we associate with historical records. Placed here, it draws on aspects of Xerxes' reign with which we are familiar and foreshadows what is to come, anticipating the impending tension and crisis.

---

1. Such interplay is often present in stories about biblical heroes. See e.g. Joseph is honoured by his father but dishonoured by his brothers and by Pharaoh. This leads to imprisonment where he meets the cupbearer and baker whose dreams relate to future honour and shame (NB the baker is also to be impaled on a tree [Gen. 40:19]). Joseph is finally honoured (he becomes second in rank, cf. Gen. 41:40 and Esth. 10:3) and acts as his people's 'saviour'.

4. HAMAN'S PLOT AGAINST THE JEWISH EXILES: 'after these things …' (Esther 3:1–15)

Context

Following the chapters of scene setting, the third chapter describes the crisis that dominates the rest of the story. The main action really begins here, although features of the preceding narrative are important to the writer's literary and ideological purposes. The crisis is a plan of genocide against the Jews that is hatched and progressed and gathers momentum in this chapter. By the end of the chapter the execution of the plan, though intentionally delayed, seems inevitable.

Contrasting with the plain reporting style of 2:19–23, the narrative becomes flamboyant again, mirroring some of the exaggeration and repetition of chapter 1, but it is less comical and more tragic, as befits its serious subject matter. In this chapter there are many examples of literary interplay that draw on earlier elements and anticipate later language, themes and style. Esther herself is notable by her absence, providing the writer with a free rein to concentrate on the introduction of his last major character – Haman – the villain and protagonist.

A. Haman's power (3:1–11)

The theme of honour provides the backdrop to these verses. Haman is honoured by a king who himself craves honour, and, by the end of verse 11, Haman has extracted for himself some of the honour tied up with the king's authority.

Comment

i. Haman's rise to power (3:1–2)

1. The chapter begins in the same way as chapter 2 (*after these events*, see comments on 2:1) as all the major English versions (except the NIV) make clear. Although the exact length of time between the events of this chapter and the preceding one is uncertain, it is clear that Esther has been queen for five years before Haman presents his plan of genocide to the king (cf. 2:16–17 and 3:7).

Like Mordecai (see comments on 2:5), Haman's name is introduced alongside descriptive elements that highlight his role in the story. He is described as *son of Hammedatha* (the exact identity of whom is unknown, but both this name and the name Haman are attested in Elamite and Persian texts). More important (as is affirmed by its reappearance in 3:10; 8:3, 5; 9:23), Haman is an *Agagite*, a term associated with the Amalekite enemies of God's people (see Exod. 17:8–16; Deut. 25:17–19; 1 Chr. 4:43). By this designation, Haman's conflict with Mordecai finds ancient roots: Mordecai, of Saul's family line (see comments on 2:5) encounters Haman (of the family line of King Agag, the king of the Amalekites), but the results for Mordecai (Esth. 10) are quite different from those experienced by Saul (1 Sam. 15).[1] From the moment of Haman's introduction, the Jewish reader would be in no doubt that Mordecai represents the redemptive presence of God among his people, whereas Haman stands in opposition to that

---

1. The term 'Agagite' came to typify all enemies of the Jews. This perhaps explains why the Greek versions identify Haman as a Bougaion (3:1) and a Macedonian (9:24). The Greek authors appear to have updated the reference 'Agagite' by these terms in order to make the enemy status of Haman more obvious in their own context.

presence. However, it is Haman and not Mordecai who is honoured, elevated and promoted to a high seat. This repeated theme in the chapter's opening sentence serves at least three purposes: (1) it shocks the reader who at the end of chapter 2 expects Mordecai to be honoured for saving the king's life; (2) it emphasizes the sense of impending danger: an enemy is in a high position (but there is hope here because this is the highest position Haman can reach, so the only way he can go is down!); (3) it anticipates the irony of Mordecai's elevation (10:3).

2. This irony is enhanced as it is in the context of describing Haman's honour that the first signs of emerging honour for Mordecai are detected. Mordecai is similar to Vashti: they both take the daring path of refusing to honour men who are unquestioningly honoured by everyone else. The results for both bring consequences personally (their integrity is established) and globally (an empire-wide crisis emerges). Note that the king has to 'command' honour for Haman: perhaps the intended implication is that commanded honour is in fact no honour at all! What is clear is that Mordecai is a threat to Haman's status: a refusal to bow down implies no sense of indebtedness or inferiority to him.

ii. Haman's anger against Mordecai (3:3–5)

These verses make sense only in the light of the deep-rooted historical ethnic enmity between the Amalekites and the Jews. It is clear that Mordecai explains his non-compliance by referring to his ethnicity; *he had told them he was a Jew*.[2]

3–4. The officials' question is both a request for a reason as well as a means of urging Mordecai to comply with expectations. The officials are persistent: they spoke with him 'day after day but he

---

2. The reason for Mordecai's non-compliance has been discussed at length in the commentaries. It has been proposed that Mordecai is obstinate; personally affronted by being overlooked for promotion; behaving like any Jew by not bowing down to any human being on religious grounds (maybe Haman even had an image of a pagan god on his chest); showing loyalty to the king because Haman had been involved in the conspiracy at the end of ch. 2. None of these reasons seem either probable or necessary in the light of the text's own clue at the end of v. 4.

would not listen' (RSV, preserving the literal translation). The Hebrew text mirrors that of Genesis 39:10, where another Jewish man in a foreign court, Joseph, refused to comply with the persistent requests of Potiphar's wife. Although the circumstances are different, the parallel is maintained because Joseph, like Mordecai, finds an outpouring of anger against him (Gen. 39:19; cf. Esth. 3:5), although both are finally honoured and become instruments of deliverance for God's people. The parallel between Mordecai and one of the great patriarchs of the Jewish faith cannot be missed.

The author points out that Haman had to be told of Mordecai's affront. Perhaps Haman is too full of his own importance to notice things for himself. It seems that the officials may have been concerned to find out whether ethnic rivalry was a justified reason for Mordecai's actions. In a Persian Empire that proudly defended ethnic diversity, the officials, far from being set against Mordecai themselves, may have had a genuine interest in the response.

5. There have already been two appearances of the word *ḥēmâ* ('rage', 1:12; 2:1) both referring to the emotions of Xerxes. Like Xerxes, Haman's rage follows a personal affront and prompts revenge of disproportionate size. It is interesting that Haman's name sounds like this Hebrew verb (often associated in the OT with fools who can expect disaster, e.g. Prov. 19:19; 27:4, 22) adding gravity to Haman's characterization.[3] Haman expresses no concern for the king's honour in that his command is violated by one of his subjects; rather he is only outraged by a personal sense of indignation.

iii. Haman plots the destruction of all the Jews (3:6–9)

6. Haman's anger at Mordecai turns into an attempt to find a genuine 'final solution' to the 'Jewish problem' (Bauckham 1989: 121).[4]

---

3. The literary symmetry between 1:12 and 3:5, and subsequently between 1:13–22 and 3:5–13, should not be missed. It underlines the author's literary skills and the links he establishes between his main characters.

4. Recognizing this, Bauckham sees parallels between Hitler's anti-Semitic plan of genocide and that of Haman in terms of origins, method and intended outcome. The existence of men like Haman is a chilling reality not an improbability today.

It is possible that Haman understood Mordecai to represent all Jewish people in standing against him. Certainly this is an opportunity for Haman to take a decisive victory in long wrangling ethnic tensions. The author uses earlier vocabulary: Haman 'scorned' the idea of limited revenge (see comments on *bzh* translated 'despise' in 1:17–18); he uses assassination terminology from 2:21 (lit. 'send out a hand against'; NIV 'killing' in 3:6), which links Haman with treacherous behaviour, and parallels a threat against the king with a threat against the Jews.[5]

7. This verse establishes two dates: the date when lots were cast (in the first month, Nisan, of Xerxes' twelfth year) and the date on which the lot fell (choosing the twelfth month, Adar). So Haman's determination to choose a lucky day meant a delay of nearly a year. The precise day of the implementation of the edict to kill the Jews is identified in verse 13 as the thirteenth day of Adar, although the edict is written down on the thirteenth day of Nisan (v. 12), allowing eleven months for distribution and necessary planning.

Additional note: the *pûr*

The use of *pûr* (the Akkadian word for small clay cubes [die] thrown to determine fate and destiny) is attested in polytheistic societies. In Persia this was a custom particularly associated with the New Year period. The Hebrew word is *gôrāl* (appearing in Esth. 3:7 by means of explanation of *pûr*). It was a common practice in the ancient world and it seems that the Israelites themselves made use of it (see Josh. 15:1ff. where the Hebrew term is used for decisions about land distribution; see also Josh. 7:18; 14:2; Ps. 16:5–6; Prov. 16:33, where the *gôrāl* is subject to God's will and purpose).

It is the appearance of the *pûr* in Esther that explains the establishment of the Jewish festival of Purim (the plural form of the Akkadian term) commemorating the events recorded in the book of Esther. As Beckett explains, the Purim festival celebrates,

---

5. The double appearance of the phrase 'the people of Mordecai', though omitted in the LXX, is perhaps a further indication that for the author Mordecai is representative of all Jews.

the chance, fate and luck of the drawing of the lot and the casting of the die ultimately in their favour, despite the intention of Haman, the rule of law, the structure of society and the apparent hopelessness of their circumstances … God chooses these very means in order to accomplish their deliverance (2002: 35).

8. Haman introduces his plan to the king by suggesting that there is a *certain people* (lit. 'one people'/'a people') who contaminate his empire and threaten his interests. There are no specific allegations, just a collection of ideas that give the impression that this people have wide influence, are guilty of disobedience, and deserve punishment. Levenson describes Haman's speech as 'a rhetorical masterpiece as subtle in its construction as it is malevolent in intent' (1997: 70). It is ironic that Haman says *it is not in the king's best interest to tolerate them* when the latest conspiracy against him was uncovered by two of their number (2:22–23). There is perhaps a second level of irony created by the use of the verb *nwḥ* (here NIV 'to tolerate'), which also occurs in 9:17, 18 and 22 (NIV 'rested/ relief'). It is a distinctive word that seems to anticipate the end of the story where the Jews are in fact granted the relief and rest that Haman here is so eager for them to be denied (see also comments on 2:18). In short, Haman's words slander the Jews by insinuation.

9. The slander is supported by a ready-to-go strategy and a monetary bribe. The king doesn't have to think: as with Memucan in chapter 1, Haman has already identified a solution – another wide-ranging decree. Again like Memucan, Haman prefixes the solution with a respectful *if it pleases the king* (cf. 1:19), at least implying that the king has authority in the matter. The amount of money offered is ridiculously excessive (possibly about two-thirds of a year's revenue from the whole empire). It seems that this echoes some of the irony and ridicule at the story's beginning. Understood as hyperbole it is unnecessary to identify the source of this money (empire resources at Haman's disposal, Haman's excessive personal wealth, money accumulated from the intended booty snatch [3:13] are all possibilities), but it is important to note that money is a persuasive and motivating factor in Persian government. It seems that Haman anticipates that loss of revenue or the cost of the operation would deter the king's co-operation, so he reassures him that money will not be a problem.

iv. Haman is now in charge (3:10–11)

Without questioning Haman further, the king gives Haman the authority and the right to do as he pleases. Either Xerxes is satisfied that Haman's planned course of action is the right one or he is simply not bothered how the Jews are handled. The 'do as you like' attitude is dismissive of the gravity of annihilating a whole people group and is arguably an indication of the delegated authority that Xerxes' honoured servant has achieved. Xerxes gives away his *signet ring*[6] and his executive power to the one again identified as *the Agagite, the enemy of the Jews*, the avenger of a personal vendetta. At this point Haman reaches his menacing peak – the tag the author assigns him is affirmed by his newly found authority to execute his plan of genocide. Furthermore, regarding the sum Haman had mentioned the king says, 'the money is given to you' (RSV, NRSV, cf. NKJV). Whether this implies acceptance of Haman's financial arrangements or a change of plan is difficult to judge (though *keep the money* [NIV] opts for the latter). What is clear is that Xerxes is handing over the matter to Haman, in whose hands resources and people are placed. The irony of the Hebrew text lies in that Haman is literally instructed to deal with the people 'as it seems good to you' (maintained by English versions except the NIV). For Haman, destruction is what 'seems good', but it is in fact evil.

Meaning

Having extracted honour and authority from Xerxes, Haman has made Xerxes nothing more than a puppet king. There is nothing in the chapter that suggests he retains the greatness and glory associated with his introduction in chapter 1. The Jewish

---

6. All major English versions translate the Hebrew (*ṭaba'aṭ*) in this way, though it should be noted that the verbal root means 'to sink', which is conveyed well by the translation 'seal', especially where it is connected with the authorizing of officials or missives (see Esth. 3:12 and cf. Gen. 41:41–42).

people themselves are silent victims of a plan that gathers pace; just like Vashti they are not consulted or allowed to speak. The passivity of the Jews (and Xerxes' virtual passivity) only serves to heighten the sense of Haman's active and controlling presence and power. There remains nothing and no one to hold the Agagite back.

B. The edict of genocide (3:12–15)

Context
The cumbersome administrative system relating to decree writing and distribution is described for a second time (cf. Esth. 1:19–22). Again the detail appears to mock the Persian system, not least because the system designed to meet the needs of a diverse populace is now used to promote the end of the Jewish facet of that diversity.

Comment

i. The edict is written (3:12)
The significance of the date (possibly part of the official text of the edict) is that it explains that the edict is written down and sealed on the eve of the Passover (thirteenth of Nisan). As the Jews are preparing to celebrate God's act of deliverance in their distant past, a present threat to their survival emerges.

There is a level of detachment here, created by a string of passive verbs. People are summoned and things are written and sealed and sent according to established procedures. There is no indication of emotion, just actions of duty. At the same time, being sealed with the king's own signet ring, there is a deathly ring of finality.

ii. The edict is distributed (3:13–15)
13–14. These verses emphasize the totality and all-inclusiveness of the edict's remit. It is all-inclusive because it is sent *to all the king's provinces* and applies to *all the Jews – young and old, women and little children*. It means total massacre, for the order is *to destroy, kill and annihilate*, which amounts to repetition for the sake of solemnity. In addition, even Jewish goods are to be plundered (see comments on 9:10, 15, 16). This mass destruction is scheduled for one day: the

thirteenth of Adar, as determined (apparently) by lot. Verse 14 adds further emphasis and repetition, clarifying that people of *every nationality* were to respond to the edict's instruction to massacre the Jews, for the edict was given as irrevocable law (*dāt*).

15. The edict was communicated far and wide, but also close at home *in the citadel of Susa*. Representative of the king's honour and glory, it is in this city that the effects of enmity are keenly felt. Whereas the king and Haman settle back to their normal routine of self-indulgence, all pretence that this is normality is denied by the city's inhabitants. They are *bewildered* (the NIV here conveys something of the highly agitated state contained in the Hebrew verb and is preferable to other translations such as 'perplexed' [NKJV, RSV]). The contrast between the king and his people is stark, and it is worth noting that the bewilderment consumes all Susa's population: other non-Jews did not react like Haman and the king. The next time the whole city is mentioned, the contrast could not be greater (see 8:15).

Meaning

The crisis point has been reached: the fate of the Jews has been sealed. Mordecai, Esther and the Jewish people have been upstaged by their most ardent enemy. The law awaits its moment of implementation and the tension is high. It is at this point in the story that the re-introduction of figures of hope is required.

5. MORDECAI AND ESTHER RESPOND TO HAMAN'S PLOT: 'when Mordecai learned ...' (Esther 4:1 – 5:8)

Context

Until this point in the story, it has been the king and his officials who have been responsible for responding to moments of crisis. Whether by personal emotional outbursts (see 1:12; 3:5) or by designing a course of action (see 1:19–22; 2:1–4; 3:8–14), their power lies in their capacity to act rather than merely accept circumstances that confront them.[1] At the end of chapter 3 the citizens of Susa are *bewildered*. Now Mordecai, representing the Jewish community of Susa and beyond, takes action that prompts other people

---

1. One possible exception to this is Mordecai's and Esther's involvement in overturning the conspiracy against the king in 2:21–23. While this hints that there was more to them than meets the eye, it was an aside to the main plot and they served as reporters rather than action takers: it was the king's court that investigated and impaled the conspirators.

too to move from helpless and passive acceptance of circumstances to a place where they can challenge and change their destiny. It has taken a crisis point of severe magnitude to mobilize and empower a subdued and reticent people, but through this mobilization the resolution of the story begins. Now the attention turns from Haman to Mordecai and then from Mordecai to Esther. It is Esther who emerges as the figure of hope upon whom the outcome of the story depends. At this point in the story she has stature of her own. She displays emotion that is real but restrained and is a determined and cunning strategist (thus mirroring but surpassing the figures of power in the king's court).

A. Esther discovers Haman's intentions (4:1–9)

Chapter 4 takes up the setting at the end of chapter 3: the king and Haman are happily drinking while Susa is bewildered, and the focus narrows (initially) to one man, Mordecai. Verses 1–9 illustrate the distance between Mordecai and Esther and between Esther and her people. They operate in different worlds and their perspectives are different from each other.

Comment

i. Mordecai weeps in sackcloth (4:1–4)

1. Mordecai leads all the Jews in an act of public mourning, displaying grief and emotion. In ancient times, as in some cultures today, demonstrating grief in this way was the norm,[2] and therefore does not imply that Mordecai was behaving in an ostentatious way.

---

2. See e.g. Gen. 37:34; 2 Sam. 1:11; 3:31; Job 2:12; Isa. 3:24; Ezek. 27:30–33; Dan 9:3. Greek historians tell us the Persians were known for tearing clothes in grief after defeats (e.g. Herodotus 8:99). Herodotus (3:117) also states that people in great need would come to the king's palace to weep for his mercy. Showing grief in this way was interpreted as a sign of repentance and humility, intending to turn away divine anger. It accompanied any experience of loss, be it through bereavement, defeat at war, or loss of personal status.

However, the wording here emphasizes that Mordecai does nothing to avert attention: he goes *into the city* (better 'through the city' [NRSV] and 'into the midst of the city' [NKJV]), *wailing loudly and crying bitterly*. The Hebrew root *z'q* ('to cry out') is repeated twice here, giving the literal sense 'and he cried out with a great and bitter crying out' (cf. NKJV retains the repetition). The same verb is used in Jonah 3:7 where the king of Ninevah 'cried out' a decree to the people urging them to fast, cover themselves with sackcloth and call on God. The parallel is interesting because the action of the Ninevites is in anticipation of coming disaster, just like the situation that Mordecai and the Jews find themselves in here. The difference is that there is no implication in Esther that those facing destruction were guilty of evil for which their mourning and fasting signified repentance. Mordecai's public display of mourning is significant because (i) it induces the Jewish community to follow his example (thus establishing Mordecai as a representative figure); and (ii) it allows Esther to become aware promptly of the threat to the Jews (enabling Esther's emergence as deliverer of her people).

2. By dressing himself in clothes of mourning, Mordecai excludes himself from access to the king's gate. As far as the story goes, this means that the barrier between Esther and Mordecai (and the Jewish people) has grown, which both adds tension and establishes Esther as ideally placed to emerge as their figure of hope. Although there is no wider evidence of a law to ban sackcloth inside the king's gate, it would be consistent with a concern for the dignity of the king's residence, especially if Herodotus' comment means that needy people often came to the palace to express distress (see fn. 2 above).

3. Mordecai's actions are copied by the Jews in *every province* when they hear 'the word of the king and his law' (lit.). Profound solemnity is conveyed by this phrase and by the synonyms *fasting, weeping and wailing* that describe the type of mourning that takes place. This list of synonyms also occurs in Joel 2:12,[3] where the context is that the prophet is urging God's people to repentance

---

3. NB The NIV translates Joel 2:12 as 'fasting and weeping and mourning', but the Hebrew verbs are identical to those in Esther.

(cf. comments on Jon. 3 above). Note that in Esther 4:14, Joel 2:14 and Jonah 3:9, these outward demonstrations of anguish are connected to the question *who knows?* In Jonah and Joel the *who knows* is related to whether God will have compassion on his people, whereas in Esther God's involvement is not mentioned at all (see comments on v. 14 below). These connections may suggest, however, that to the Jewish mind acts of corporate mourning are always associated with repentance and entreating God to intervene with compassion.

4. Whether or not Esther's personal servants knew the details of her relationship with Mordecai, it seems that they knew she would be interested in his welfare. Esther appears to be on good terms with those around her (just as she had been with Hegai). Although Esther is oblivious to the reason for Mordecai's behaviour, she has the insight to know that something serious is afoot because she responds in *great distress*. The word is an unusual form of the verb *ḥyl*, which is used to describe a physical response to pain or anguish (cf. Job 15:20 and Jer. 23:9). With the additional adverb here it conveys the sense of 'greatly writhing in pain'. This description of Esther's response to Mordecai's mourning suggests that by sending Mordecai a new set of clothes Esther does not want a quick fix to Mordecai's unseemly behaviour, but instead she wishes Mordecai to dress in a way that would qualify him for entry into the king's gate again. However, Mordecai refuses to take the clothes, and again the author leaves us to wonder why (cf. Mordecai's refusal to bow to Haman in Esth. 3:2). The effect of this verse is to emphasize the distance between Mordecai and Esther once more: she does not go and he does not come closer. Instead they communicate at a distance through intermediaries. In the light of the widespread knowledge of Haman's edict in verse 3, it seems remarkable that Esther and her servants seem oblivious to its existence. However, the separation of court life from reality has already been established (e.g. Esth. 1:1–9; 2:12–16; 3:15).

ii. Esther investigates through Hathach (4:5–9)

Though limited by her situation, Esther begins to take action at her own initiative: she sends clothes and then she sends Hathach. This pro-activity is the start of Esther assuming control.

5. Esther 'calls' (NIV *summoned*) and then 'commands' (NIV *ordered*) Hathach to *find out* (NRSV 'to learn') what was going on. Hathach's task is to learn what was going on, just as Mordecai had done (v. 1).[4] Hathach is commissioned to learn 'the why and the wherefore of it all' (Berlin, 2001: 46), which nicely expresses a level of bewilderment consistent with the story's emphasis. When Hathach conveys the results of his investigation to Esther, she will have the same insight as Mordecai himself.

6. The meeting between Hathach and Mordecai takes place in a very public space in front of the king's gate. The *open square* (NIV) is the place specified in 6:9 and 11 where Mordecai will be honoured by the king. The contrast could not be greater between Mordecai's present sackcloth clothing and the future robes of honour he will wear.[5]

7. Mordecai holds nothing back from Hathach. By the words *everything that had happened to him* Mordecai hints that from his perspective the crisis had started with him and he was still at its centre. Once more Mordecai has learned every last detail (cf. v. 5 above and 2:22), including details of Haman's bribe money (used in the story to underline Haman's treachery, cf. 7:4).[6]

8. To his account of the story Mordecai adds an official copy of the written edict and a personal plea to Esther. The official copy is presumably to be shown to inform her of all the details. The personal plea comes in a series of instructions: Mordecai tells

---

4. All the main versions (except NIV) retain the parallelism established by the use of the Hebrew verb *yd'* ('to know') in both vv. 1 and 5.

5. The identical location is lost in the NIV, which identifies the location in 6:9 and 11 as the city streets. The RSV/NRSV is more consistent in this instance, translating all three identical Hebrew phrases by 'in the open square of the city'.

6. The meaning of the Hebrew word *pārāšâ* (NIV 'exact') is not certain. Levenson (1997: 77–78) translates it as 'story' on the basis of its meaning in 10:2 and other post-biblical sources where it means 'full account', 'passage' or 'text'. The verbal form is used in Lev. 24:12, where it seems to mean 'to clarify' or 'to make distinct', which is closer to the NIV here.

Hathach to *urge* (the verb means 'to command') Esther to go, to implore and to seek mercy from the king 'concerning her people'. Mordecai is asking Esther to forget his previous instruction to hide her identity and to risk all by identifying with the Jews. The challenge Esther faces is not dissimilar to the one faced by Moses, another Jew, who also found himself in a privileged position within a foreign set-up and was told to go, in his case to the Egyptian Pharaoh, for the sake of his people (see Exod. 3:10). It is significant that this is the last time Mordecai tells Esther what to do – the indirect nature of the instructions here hints that their relationship is changing.

9. Hathach's loyalty is reiterated by the plain statement that he completed the assignment Esther had set for him and reports back faithfully to her. Note Esther and Mordecai rely on the services of a straightforward servant who is rather different from the manipulative men who surround Xerxes.

Meaning

While nothing is guaranteed for the Jews, there is hope on the horizon, because at least Esther has established indirect communication with Mordecai and is 'in the know' like Mordecai and her people as a whole. She has shown initiative in obtaining this knowledge but the tension remains: will Esther take up the challenge Mordecai has set before her?

B. Mordecai enlists Esther's help (4:10–17)

Context

Verse 10 marks a change from indirect speech to direct speech. Although intermediaries are still necessary, the actual words Mordecai and Esther speak are now recorded in a way that heightens the drama. It is as if Mordecai and Esther's cause depends on every word uttered between them. These verses also mark a dramatic change in the characterization of Esther. She develops new maturity and exhibits fearless determination, as she takes up Mordecai's challenge, and the moment of crisis resolution draws closer.

Comment

i. Esther's unenviable position (4:10–11)

These verses make two things clear. First, Esther has enough authority to command her servant Hathach to return to Mordecai
with another message (v. 10); second, her authority in the king's
court is no greater than that of any other of his subjects (v. 11).
This is both her predicament and her opportunity. Her words
explain her precarious situation to Mordecai. He needs to know
that the king has not recently shown her any of the favour she originally received (cf. 2:15–16), and therefore she can expect only the
death penalty (just like any other *man or woman*) if she goes into the
king as Mordecai has suggested. Esther does not disobey Mordecai,
but she does 'argue the impossibility of compliance' (Fox, 1991:
61). This is the first time in the story that she dares to question
Mordecai's wisdom. On the surface Esther seems at pains to indicate to Mordecai that she may not be the solution he thinks she is
– after all, Vashti was deposed for breaking the king's law and
Esther can expect no better treatment. But Esther mentions the
possibility of the king making an exception by holding out his gold
sceptre,[7] so there is an element of hope. Maybe the beginnings of
a plan are forming in Esther's mind, although she doesn't under-
estimate its danger.[8]

ii. Mordecai challenges Esther (4:12–14)

Mordecai's response to Esther has three elements: (1) her own life
is in danger; (2) the Jews will be saved with or without her; (3) her

---

7. Yamauchi (1990: 360–361) describes two treasury reliefs from
   Persepolis that show a Persian king with a gold staff (sceptre) in his
   right hand.

8. Esther's words have been compared with Moses' words of hesitation
   when he is asked to go to Pharaoh. The difference here is that even if
   Esther is objecting to Mordecai's instructions, she does so on the
   basis of the danger that it places her in, rather than out of a sense of
   unworthiness that underpins Moses' hesitations (see Exod. 3 and 4 and
   comments on 4:8 above).

very purpose in life is at stake. Although Mordecai's words are sometimes understood as a veiled or open threat, it is more consistent
with the role Mordecai assumes in the story to conclude that he is
simply advising Esther that it is better for her to act than not to act.
By so doing, she secures at least the possibility of self-survival. In
other words, Mordecai is still acting as her protective guardian. He
also reminds Esther of her Jewish roots twice (vv. 13 and 14),
repeating the emphasis at the end of verse 8.

It has often been argued that Mordecai expresses his belief that
God will intervene if Esther does not by saying *relief and deliverance
for the Jews will arise from another place.* This seems unhelpful because
it supposes that Esther can keep God out of his people's story!
The phrase may imply that if Esther does not respond to her
people's need, God will raise up someone else, but the omission
of any reference to God means that we add to the text this theological perspective. Bauckham's comment is instructive:

> Mordecai does not mean that if Esther does not do something, God
> will. He means that deliverance for the Jews will occur somehow,
> whether through Esther's actions or some other means … His 'who
> knows whether …?' is not scepticism, but nor has it the confidence of
> prophecy. It is a hopeful working hypothesis.[9]

The author seems to be at pains to refrain from mentioning God
in this most important of all Mordecai's speeches. It is arguably
more difficult to keep God out here than to include him, but the
latter would conflict with the author's overriding purpose (see
Introduction, p. 48f. and comments on 4:3 above).

What is clear is that Mordecai's speech is inspirational and effective. Mordecai underestimates neither the severity of Esther's
predicament nor the saving qualities of her potential. He motivates
and mobilizes Esther for action.

iii. Esther accepts her role (4:15–17)

15–16. Without hesitation, Esther now takes up the challenge.

---

9. Bauckham 1989: 125.

She both anticipates her life's course and accepts her life's purpose at this defining moment. In this context, Esther's commitment (rather than her fatalism) is expressed by the phrase *if I perish, I perish*, but the dramatic tension is increased by this statement of intent.[10]

Esther requests that the Jewish people identify themselves with her through fasting, just as she has identified herself with them by taking up their cause. No longer is she ignorant of their circumstances for she now acts with them. She instructs Mordecai to gather all the Jews in Susa to fast on her behalf (NRSV, cf. NIV *for me*), indicating her own centrality in the emerging plan to secure their survival. The fast exceeds expected norms, being of three days duration (rather than just one) and extending across all hours of the day and night. The severity of the fast matches the severity of the situation and serves to emphasize the solidarity of the people with their representative. There is no indication that the fast assumed religious significance, although Greek texts add that it was accompanied by prayer.[11]

17. The chapter ends with a clear indication that Esther is assuming responsibility for the Jewish people at this moment of their greatest crisis. Providing a stark contrast to what has gone before (e.g. 2:20), Mordecai now carries out Esther's instructions.

Meaning
Hope for the hopeless has emerged in the form of a courageous and sensible young woman, who unfortunately considers herself

---

10. Cf. Gen. 43:14 where a similar phrase is used by Jacob to express his commitment to a course of action fraught with danger but to which no real alternative exists.

11. For a discussion on fasting in OT times, see Baldwin (1984: 81–85). Note that the omission of words of prayer at this moment of crisis is consistent with the reality of human experience. How easy is it to vocalize prayers at moments of real crisis? If prayer is about conforming to God's will, then Esther herself becomes the prayer of the Jews (see Beckett 2002: 49).

out of favour with the people that matter. The Jews are not out of the woods yet but there is a glimmer of light. In a perplexing way, God is most present and most absent in this chapter in which his presence seems to be suppressed. In this critical scene where questions of destiny meet human response, the author appears most 'hard-pressed to write God out of the story' (Berlin 2001: 44). As Mordecai leaves the palace environs, Esther assumes centre-stage.

C. Esther hosts a banquet (5:1–8)

Context
The scene changes dramatically once again. From the Jewish world of fasting and mourning, the reader is taken back to the courtroom of the king where feasting, not fasting, is the order of the day. Unlike the impetuous plans previously implemented, Esther's manoeuvres are paced and planned most carefully. There is no sense that events run away with themselves. Instead the pace is slow, even deliberately ponderous, as Esther introduces delay tactics to the uncovering of her plan. This means that suspense and intrigue are introduced. The reader, like Xerxes and Haman, has little idea of what is going on in Esther's head, but suspect that plenty is! Although Mordecai is mentioned in chapters 5 – 7, he makes no verbal contribution. The fact that he is silenced in these central chapters underlines the author's intention to elevate Esther as the story's heroine.

Comment

i. Esther issues the invitation (5:1–5)
   1. The opening phrase *on the third day* connects this narrative with the previous one and means Esther's approach to the king coincides with the third day of the Jewish fast. The Hebrew word *malkût* ('royalty') is used three times in this verse. Esther literally 'puts on royalty' and Xerxes sits on 'his throne of royalty' in 'the house of royalty'. The verse also refers to Xerxes three times as 'the king' (*melek*). The emphasis could not be clearer: Esther is entering her other world, the king's territory. As she does, she enters cautiously and dresses appropriately. There is no indication that

she goes through the beauty preparations described in chapter 2 for this audience with the king. She is no longer relying on her beauty or powers of seduction; instead she stands with all the dignity of a royal Jew. Note that Esther 'stops' (NIV *stood*) in the inner court; she does not at this stage approach the king. She is heeding her own warning (4:11).

2. Esther is received by the king as the exception to the rule. There have been enough hints in the story that this could have gone either way for Esther: Esther has the ability to win favour, but Xerxes is a volatile man. The possibility of such extreme and opposing outcomes means the reader is relieved, surprised and not surprised all at once by Esther's acceptance. In chapter 1, Xerxes' actions in his court were all about displaying his honour to others. Here Xerxes himself does the seeing, and Esther, not Xerxes, wins the honour. By means of a formal ceremony permitting a royal audience, Esther approaches the king.

3. It seems appropriate that the king asks Esther what she wants in the light of her unusually bold move to get herself noticed. His question is literally 'what is to you?' He does not seem to recognize Esther's distress, but rather simply expects a request. She has not been called 'Queen Esther' since chapter 2, but now Xerxes addresses her in this formal way. His offer that she could be given *even up to half the kingdom* is probably a conventional phrase, indicating that the supplicant can expect generosity and should express their request with confidence. Coming from Xerxes' lips, it is reminiscent of the 'have what you like, do as you please' mentality already exhibited towards Haman (3:10–11).[12]

4. The stage has been set for a climactic moment. The reader expects Esther to make an immediate move to save the Jewish people. Instead Esther's response is a dramatic anti-climax. She begins with the expected flattery (cf. Haman's approach to getting what he wants, 3:9) but then invites Xerxes, along with Haman, to a banquet. It seems that the author wants us to understand that Esther is biding her time rather than losing her nerve. After all, having read the edict of annihilation for herself, she knows she has

---

12. Cf. Herod's response to the daughter of Herodias in Mark 6:23.

time to play with (see comments on 3:13). Esther also adds flattery to flattery by suggesting she wants to honour Xerxes with a banquet. By so doing she surpasses any flattery Haman has ever afforded him. In chapter 1, Xerxes had to put on a banquet to applaud himself as a means of self-honouring. Esther here offers him the more meaningful honour that comes by other people's recognition. She also makes refusal almost impossible by indicating that she has already prepared this banquet.

5. Nothing works as well as pandering to Xerxes' ego, and Xerxes consents immediately. He gives instructions for Haman to come immediately, which is the first time Haman comes under the authority of Esther's wishes. In 3:15 'the word of the king' (*děbar hammelek*) signified the king's authoritative command (see also 5:8). Here Xerxes does not hesitate to refer to 'the word of Esther' (*děbar 'estēr*). The toning down to *what Esther asks* (NIV; cf. NRSV 'as Esther desires') seems to underplay the significance of Esther's role at this juncture.

ii. The banquet is held and a further invitation is issued (5:5–8)
Halfway through verse 5 the words 'so the king and Haman came' (NRSV) indicate that there is a transition in the story to the new setting: Esther's banquet.

6. During the wine course (presumably at the end of the banquet), Xerxes asks Esther again what he can do for her, mirroring the sentiments of verse 3 in a slightly prolonged way. It is perhaps significant in the light of the fact that Vashti lost all when the king was drinking wine (1:10–12) that Esther again chooses to respond with delay tactics.

7. This verse simply reads 'Esther answered and said, "My petition and request …"' There is nothing equivalent to the 'this is' that is placed either at the beginning or end of the verse in English versions. The sense seems to be that Esther begins to answer and then breaks off and doesn't answer, perhaps enticing the king's curiosity rather than losing her confidence.

8. Using Xerxes' own words in the next stage of her response, Esther invites Xerxes and Haman to a further banquet on the following day. She indicates that this is when she will make her request known and implies that she has confidence because she believes the king wishes to fulfil her request for she has found favour in his eyes. There is an interesting twist here because the writer of the story always refers to Esther 'winning' favour in an active sense. In her wisdom and deference Esther presents herself as passive: she 'finds' favour; it is given to her rather than extracted by her. As Bush explains, 'Esther is shrewdly and subtly pursuing a well-designed plan by which she has manoeuvred the king into committing himself in advance' (1996: 407). Esther ends by placing herself under the authority of the king's word (cf. comments on 5:5 above), implying that the second banquet invitation is part of her compliance to the king.

Meaning

The first part of chapter 5 affirms beyond doubt that events are now under Esther's control. She dictates their timing and the manner of their execution. In terms of the story's design, her endless delay tactics increase tension and suspense; in terms of its outcome, it secures the necessary conditions for reversal.

Ever since the crisis took hold at the start of chapter 4, Esther's character has been taking on new dimensions. She has accepted that her identity and destiny are tied up with that of her people and she cannot escape the impact of that. Her life will be changed and she will be the one to change it.

But now before the crisis can be resolved, a further delay is introduced, not by Esther, but by the writer's decision to interrupt the developing story-line with a complicating episode. It serves to remind the reader that the honour of attending royal banquets can only provide momentary escapism for men like Haman.

6. HAMAN'S PLOT AGAINST MORDECAI:
'filled with rage against Mordecai' (Esther 5:9–14)

Context

This episode occurs immediately after Esther's first banquet. The reader expects the second banquet, and Esther's accompanying climactic request, to follow immediately. In one sense, therefore, Esther 5:9 – 6:14 interrupts the main plot and extends the tension and suspense. But the reader's interest in the related subplot, the conflict between Mordecai and Haman, has already been nurtured, and this episode resumes the themes and structure of 3:1–6. Just as was the case in chapter 3, Esther is kept out of 5:9 – 6:14. Her absence is surprising, given the fact that she is in control in the first part of chapter 5, but the scheduling of the second banquet for 'tomorrow' excuses Esther from the events of the rest of the day.

It is significant that chapters 5 – 7 use the banquet motif. Esther 5:9 describes Haman leaving a banquet in a cheerful state. In Esther 6:14, Haman is whisked off to another banquet with his wife's chilling words resounding over his life. Joy is short-lived for a man like Haman: the ups and downs of his emotional life are illustrated in these two very different episodes (5:9–14; 6:1–14), which both rely on Haman's self-obsession.

A. Haman's emotional turmoil (5:9–13)

These verses heighten the tension and reinforce the characterization of Haman. Once more he emerges as an egocentric megalomaniac bent on retaliation and destruction if his fragile ego is subject to the slightest provocation. This provides a contrast to Esther, who with reluctance has taken up a cause for the purpose of saving others, and Mordecai, who shows total disregard for self-preservation. There is irony too, because Haman plans to gain honour through dishonouring Mordecai, whereas Mordecai dishonours Haman but finds Haman is required to honour him (ch. 6).

Comment

9. The extreme contrast in Haman's emotions in this verse is related to him being honoured (as a guest of the queen) and then dishonoured (by a Jew such as Mordecai). He leaves the banquet (after the wine course, v. 6) *happy and in high spirits* (cf. Xerxes, see comments on 1:10), suggesting he is both merry and feeling rather pleased with himself. As Weisman explains, Haman is 'giddy with the gesture of warmth and respect shown to him by Esther' (1998: 151). The single man Mordecai is again able to destroy Haman's satisfaction in an instant (cf. 3:2–5). It seems that Mordecai's response to Haman is now even more disdainful than his previous reaction: he now doesn't even stand up or shake before Haman, let alone bow down (cf. 3:2). The Hebrew verb *zw'* means 'to move or quake with fear' and is used to describe the reaction of someone in the presence of a powerful superior. It is this respect related to his royal appointment that Mordecai refuses to recognize. The author reports Haman's reaction by using exactly the same words as those that occur in 3:5: 'Haman was filled with rage' (NRSV retains the parallel in both verses by the words 'He/Haman was infuriated').

10. It seems out of character that Haman *restrained himself.*[1] Whether Haman decided not to react out of fear of giving Mordecai's act further publicity (pretending not to notice Mordecai or be perturbed by him), or whether Haman was completely flummoxed about what his next move should be, is uncertain. What is clear is that his lack of immediate public response does not imply a measured, internal response. Haman's indignation adds further tension to the sub-plot and, because we don't know what Haman plans to do about it, the tension is heightened. Haman decides to go home, and as he does so, the first glimpses are seen of the influences on Haman – his friends (also called 'advisers/wise men', suggesting an official role, 6:13; cf. 1:13) and his wife Zeresh. Haman gathers his supporters around him to bolster his confidence (a little like Esther herself asked Mordecai to do on her behalf at the end of ch. 4).

11. Although Haman clearly *boasted* (NIV) to his friends and his wife, it is a form of the verb *spr* (meaning 'to relate/to recount') that is used (hence NKJV 'told' and NRSV 'recounted'). The original meaning brings a greater sense of irony than the NIV here, because Haman is found to be gathering people around him to tell them things they already know. This is particularly realistic, as merriment often produces this sort of unnecessary behaviour. Haman speaks about 'the glory of his wealth' (in preference to NIV *his vast wealth*), his many sons, how the king had made him great and how the king had 'lifted him up' above his other officials. In this short summary things that really matter to Haman are emphasized. They are the same things as those that matter to Xerxes (cf. 1:4) and are essentially wealth, recognition and abundance. The emphasis here is highly ironic, anticipating the outcome of the story whereby Haman's riches are given to Esther (8:1) and his sons are killed by the Jews (9:10).

12. Haman's final claim to honour is that Esther has honoured only him alongside the king. Here the irony reaches its climax:

---

1. The same verb is used in Gen. 43:31 and 45:1 to describe Joseph who 'restrains himself' before his brothers, also conveying the idea of biding time.

Haman feels most greatly honoured because the queen has invited him to two banquets. It is of course the second banquet that provides the setting for his disgrace at Esther's hands. In referring to Esther's favour to him, Haman unwittingly confirms her authority: he recognizes that Esther has 'summoned' him (cf. Esther summoning Hathach in 4:5) and he is not in a position to refuse her invitation.

13. The thorn in Haman's egocentric flesh is of course Mordecai. Even though Haman does not relate the details of the most recent incident to his supporters, he is unable to refrain from referring with disdain to *that Jew Mordecai*. Haman indicates that he has *no satisfaction* because Mordecai is still sitting at the king's gate. The exact meaning of *šōweh* is difficult to determine. It is used in different ways within the book of Esther (see 3:8 and 7:4), but each occurrence implies a lack of benefit. It conveys com-parison and preceded by the negative means 'is not compar-able with/equivalent for' (cf. Prov. 3:15). Haman's use of the word indicates that from his perspective he receives no sense of pleasure from those things that should bring him honour, because Mordecai's dishonouring of him means too much to him in com-parison. In one sense this is ludicrous; in another it betrays the deep-rooted nature of the enmity between them (see comments on 2:5 and 3:1).

B. Haman accepts his wife's (and friends') advice to hang Mordecai (5:14)

14. The response of Zeresh (and friends) to her husband's description of the effect Mordecai has on him is shocking because it is so disproportionate. Given the fact that there is a history to the enmity between Mordecai and Haman, it is possible that Zeresh responds in this way because she is exasperated that a man as apparently insignificant as Mordecai continuously plagues Haman.

The use of gallows for hanging bodies is mentioned frequently in Esther (see 2:23; cf. 6:4; 7:9–10; 8:7; 9:13, 25), and as a final act of disgracing Mordecai it would end the battle for honour between the two enemies with a defining win for Haman (see comments on 2:23). The proposed height of the gallows – over twenty-two metres – is both absurd and impractical.[2] Maybe Zeresh didn't intend the height to be taken literally, but meant that the gallows' towering height should be visible over the whole of Susa. Alternatively, the author may have deliberately put such exaggerated measurements in Zeresh's mouth in order to mock the ludicrous nature of her suggestion.

The verse is full of ironic contrast and surprise. Haman is encouraged to carry out murder and impalement and then to dine and be happy. Haman greets an evil plan with 'delight'. He takes advice from his wife and friends, leaving the reader with the distinct impression that he has little control over his own household, contravening the king's earlier edict (see comments on 1:22). This becomes the moment of his greatest folly and the cause of his downfall. In his haste he has the gallows built to end a personal feud that would have been resolved by the edict to kill the Jews anyway, if Haman's patience had allowed the waiting time to lapse.

Meaning

The dramatic tension is increased because, while Esther takes time out to prepare another banquet, Haman plans to kill Mordecai, and both are scheduled for the following day. Both Haman and Esther need to secure an audience with the king, but for now the momentum lies with Haman. As far as we can tell, Esther is unaware of the imminent danger facing Mordecai – while the reader senses the urgency, Esther is biding her time. However, two murderous plans from Haman present two opportunities for reversal and two opportunities to double Haman's shame. Haman has the power and inclination to act in evil ways, but he has no power over the unpredictable occurrence of coincidence (ch. 6), nor the inclination to presume that Esther's power surpasses his own (ch. 7).

---

2. Cf. the height of Nebuchadnezzar's image in Dan. 3:1 (4.5 metres) and archaeological evidence that the palaces in Susa were no taller than about 14 metres.

7. XERXES HONOURS MORDECAI:
'the man the king delights to honour' (Esther 6:1–11)

Context

Chapter 6 contains the second of two episodes that intervene between the first and second banquets of Esther. It therefore prolongs suspense but it also resolves previous elements and anticipates future elements in the story. In particular, it resolves the incongruity that Mordecai was not rewarded for his earlier act of loyalty to the king (2:19–23) and deals with the recently raised tension between Haman and Mordecai (5:9–14). It anticipates coming events because this chapter is the turning point of the narrative: from these events onwards the fortunes of the Jewish people as a whole will change for the better, and Mordecai's honour here prefigures that corporate experience.

The chapter has been described as 'the most ironically comic scene in the entire Bible' (Jobes 1999: 152) and 'one of the funniest anywhere in the Bible' (Berlin 2001: 56). It presents a vivid drama where the rivalry and tension between two main characters is visibly acted out. The irony is not without purpose. It marks the place where, for the first time, the scales tip in favour of Mordecai against Haman. The irony is necessary in order to emphasize the unlikely nature of this outcome, which is secured through unexpected and unplanned coincidences.

A number of contrasting themes reach their climax here: shame versus honour, planning versus coincidence, desiring versus deserving. It is the previously exalted Haman who is the butt of the prolonged joke: he plans to titillate his desire for royal-like honour, but he receives nothing but extreme humiliation. He who has previously delighted in his peak (5:14) finds he has only devised his own downfall.

Comment

A. Mordecai's loyalty is remembered (6:1–3)

1. Xerxes could not sleep, *that night*. Note the parallel with 5:9 *that day,* emphasizing the closely related timing of these episodes. In earlier sections of the Esther narrative, months, years and days have passed between events. Now we are at the heart of the story, the passing of time is slowed down as every detail of the event is recalled. The slow passing of time indicates the centrality of these chapters in the overall scheme of the story. The Hebrew author does not explain why Xerxes couldn't sleep, although his choice of words 'the sleep of the king fled' (lit.) may hint at the line taken by the Greek translations, 'the Lord kept sleep away from the king'.[1] In the Hebrew text the king's insomnia is the first unexplained coincidence.

The Persian predilection for record keeping has already been referred to (2:23), so the reader is aware that Mordecai's name figures in these records. These references anticipate the final reference in Esther 10:2 to the *greatness of Mordecai* being written down in court records. The present reference to these court records contains two separate construct phrases usually understood to

---

1. Cf. the Aramaic phrase used in Dan. 6:18 (MT: Dan. 6:19), indicating that sleep fled from Darius.

mean 'the book of memoranda' and 'the events of the days'. It is the addition of the Hebrew word *hazzikrōnôt* (from the root *zkr* meaning 'to remember') which is the new element here, compared with the thirty or so other uses of the phrase in the OT. Bush (1996: 411) has argued that this is less likely to mean 'memorable/notable', and more likely to indicate that the king is looking at recent/current events rather than history long since past. This certainly makes sense of the present use of the term. It is unclear whether Xerxes expected this night-time reading to send him back to sleep or whether he, possibly enticed by Esther's pending revelation, had given up on sleep for the night.

2. The second coincidence is that the reader of the records reads the incident recorded in 2:21–23 (see comments). Although the identity of the first conspirator is clearly the same as that of 2:21, his name is spelt slightly differently here ('Bigthana' replaces 'Bigthan'; see RSV, NRSV, NKJV, although NIV translates both references consistently as *Bigthana*).

3. Xerxes is immediately perturbed by the fact that he has not rewarded Mordecai for his loyalty. He asks, *What honour and recognition has Mordecai received …?* These two concepts were used to describe Xerxes' own glory in 1:4. It was common practice for Persian kings to share their own privileges with those who proved themselves loyal. When Persian kings singled out benefactors for privilege, it seems that this was an opportunity to display the king's generosity as much as it was an opportunity for rewarding a deserving individual. (For further discussion, see Laniak 1998: 104–107). It seems likely that Xerxes was supported by personal attendants all hours of the day and night, to assist him as necessary. Here they are required to give him information; in 2:2 they offered him advice.

B. Xerxes takes advice from Haman (6:4–9)

The humour in this interchange between Xerxes and his most trusted adviser is built upon the combination of further coincidences and the fact that the readers know more about what is going on than the characters do themselves.

4–5. Just at the time when Xerxes is considering how to reward Mordecai with suitable honour and recognition, by coincidence

Haman enters the court. There is nothing in the text to suggest that night-time has passed and that Haman has kept to his wife's advice to go to the king in the morning (5:14). It seems that Haman takes up a position very similar to that taken by Esther when she wanted an audience with the king (5:1), but this time there is no need for a gold sceptre (cf. 5:2). But neither does the king ask Haman what he wants (cf. 5:3). The king is blissfully unaware of Haman's purpose, just as Haman is unaware of Xerxes' consuming dilemma. For the reader's benefit, just in case the situational irony is missed, the author states plainly why Haman has come: to tell the king about his plans to impale Mordecai. The providential nature of Haman's appearance at this very moment when the king needs advice is emphasized in the text by the formal introduction Haman is given by the king's attendants: 'Behold Haman is standing in the court' (see NKJV).

6. The height of the dramatic irony is reached here through what the king does not say to Haman and what Haman does not say to Xerxes. The reader, privy to both Xerxes' intentions and Haman's thought processes, sees their conversation in a different light than they both do. The king does not mention Mordecai's name as the intended beneficiary; neither does he repeat the word *recognition* (or 'promotion') which he used to his attendants (v. 3). As already a promoted man, Haman might have presumed that Xerxes did not mean him if he had used the term *recognition* here. Although he has in fact been honoured (3:1), he is of course 'a glutton for honour' (Berlin 2001: 56) and Xerxes' curtailed question whets his insatiable appetite for honour. It is possible that Xerxes is actually setting Haman up here. Such an interpretation provides an interesting angle on Haman and Xerxes' relationship and adds support to a sarcastic reading of Xerxes' words in verse 10. Haman's own thoughts are consistent with his pride and self-obsession and set up the forthcoming scene based on this 'comic misunderstanding of enormous proportion' (Berlin, ibid.). Haman's response to the king shows little understanding of the king's priority to reward someone who deserves, rather than desires, honour. However, the grand and public scale of the honours Haman suggests does indicate that he fully appreciates the king's predilection for an audience to witness his generosity (see comments on v. 4). Haman, it appears, is conceited but not dim-witted.

7. Haman's reply begins by repeating the king's words, but then breaks off in mid-sentence (cf. comments on Esther's similar way of responding to the king in 5:7, though Haman does not continue with the flattery that Esther uses, 5:8). Haman's repetition of the king's words would certainly help him to savour their meaning. This seems to be the moment that Haman has been waiting for, and, by breaking off in mid-sentence, he reaches a dramatic pause before he gets carried away and his suggestion pours out.

8–9. For Haman, honour means royalty, and so it is not surprising that his suggestion includes so many references to 'king' (*melek*) and 'royalty' (*malkût*) that the reader trips over them. It is ironic that in an environment where riches, land or position might be given to benefactors, Haman's utmost desire is for a moment of glory and a passing experience of public prestige. To some extent his plan therefore underplays expectations, but in reality Haman is asking for royalty and all its trappings and thereby surpasses expected norms. An interesting biblical precedent for rewarding loyalty is found in Genesis 41:42–43, where Joseph is similarly dressed in royal robes and publicly acclaimed. Haman's suggestion, however, surpasses the description of Joseph's moment of glory. Haman wants to wear a royal robe that the king has actually worn and ride a horse he has ridden,[2] with *one of the king's most noble princes* in attendance. All this amounts to something comparable to a bid for the throne and perhaps legitimizes an understanding of 2:21–23 that includes Haman's involvement and explains Mordecai's response to him (3:2). As it turns out, Haman's suggestion of an accompanying noble backfires, as it necessitates his own involvement in a different role to that which he expected. The location of all this activity in 'the open square of the city' (NRSV, cf. NIV *the city streets*; see comments on 4:6) suggests that Haman planned his finest moment to take place directly in front of

2. Greek writers confirm that wearing a king's robe conferred royalty (e.g. at coronation ceremonies, cf. Solomon's coronation as David's successor [1 Kgs 1:29–35]). On other occasions, usurpers put on king's

Mordecai as he sat in front of the king's gate. It appears the old enmity has not been forgotten amid his present enthusiasm. The thought of Mordecai embitters even the best moments of his life, and every moment is an opportunity to score a proverbial point.

C. Mordecai is publicly honoured (6:10–11)

10. If the king knows of the enmity between Haman and Mordecai, he certainly does not let it show. He simply accepts Haman's advice without hesitation and tells him to implement it, and then identifies Mordecai as the honouree. Xerxes refers to Mordecai as *the Jew who sits at the king's gate*, repeating the words spoken in less appreciative terms by Haman himself (5:13). From Xerxes' point of view Mordecai is no threat – he may have been more reluctant to accept this advice if Haman had been the object of his intentions! Haman is told to act quickly (cf. the use of the root *mhr* 'to make haste' in 5:5) and by this Haman is equally swiftly put in his place. All ideas of grandeur can be forgotten.

11. The climax to this episode is recorded without reference to the thoughts or feelings of Haman or Mordecai. Nothing needs to be said because the enmity and bitterness between them has already been established. The writer can trust the reader to read between the lines. Haman's plans have been curtailed by those of the king. He has not been granted a moment to make his move against Mordecai, but, on the contrary, he has been given every opportunity and every royal facility to enhance Mordecai's public honour.

Meaning
The irony in this chapter is multi-dimensional and multi-purpose. It is visibly enacted and, in its obviousness, it contrasts with the more subtle hints and impressions of irony in earlier sections of

---

robes. Archaeological evidence suggests that the horses of Persian kings were decorated with a royal crown/crest. This means that the NIV rendition is preferable to the NKJV, which gives the impression that the crown is the king's royal crown rather than the crest worn by the king's horses.

the story. The scene with which the episode ends is farcical but also acutely symbolic of a deeper reality. It has been reached by coincidences that have been carefully crafted and left unexplained. It marks the beginning of a series of reversals in favour of the Jews by empowering their representative Mordecai and humiliating their enemy Haman. The irony relies on misunderstanding and confusion that is entwined in the event but resolved at its conclusion. The resolution means that Haman is humiliated, though the king never intended that, and Mordecai is raised to royal status, though the king never really intended that either. The incident is highly illustrative of the old adage that pride comes before a fall, and anticipates the story's outcome. The reader still awaits Esther's second banquet, but while the suspense is prolonged, the agony is not. By the time Esther is reintroduced, a positive outcome for the Jews is already visible.

The chapter is reminiscent of a previous one (see comments on the meaning of ch. 4) in that it would have been an excellent opportunity for the writer to introduce religious motifs by explaining that God's hand is the unidentified hand of coincidence and reversal. However, at this critical moment in the story, such an admission would again spell out what the writer wants to keep implicit. The author is keen to allow the reader to interpret the story's events.

8. PARTIAL SUCCESS: THE DEATH OF HAMAN (Esther 6:12 – 7:10)

Context

Chapter 6 mirrors chapter 5 and ends with a similar progression of events. Mordecai dents Haman's pride, so Haman returns to the security of his own home (5:10; 6:12). But the advice he receives is different on this second occasion: on the first there was room for optimism as long as Mordecai was dealt with, but this second time he returns home to find that only pessimism remains. The intervening event, the honouring of Mordecai, has put a different perspective on things. Intensifying the indignity, the author chooses to predict Haman's downfall by the words of his wife and advisers.

If chapter 6 is the turning point of the story, then chapter 7 is perhaps its heart (Beckett 2002: 77). Irony and coincidence continue along with a number of other tension-raising devices, such as double meanings, sharp-edged phrases, unexplained pauses and farcical elements. The scheduling of events is tight, with one event, revelation or decision building the foundation for the next.

The characterization of Esther is developed in this section, as her passivity and reticence give way to forceful pro-activity. As she rises, Haman falls (fulfilling his wife's prediction) from honour to shame (mourning), reversing Mordecai's movement from shame (mourning) to honour in chapter 6. Esther's achievements in chapter 7 are the first stage in her two-stage mission: she deals with Haman (and saves Mordecai from the gallows), but she still needs to deal with the edict (and save her people from annihilation, chapter 8).

Comment

A. Haman's demise: 'you will surely fall …' (6:12 – 7:6)

i. Zeresh and advisers predict Haman's downfall (6:12–14)

12. Despite the dramatic nature of the preceding event, Mordecai and Haman immediately return to their normal walks of life. The author does not disclose how Mordecai felt about his honouring, though perhaps Bechtel hits the mark commenting, 'However sweet the taste of his temporary exaltation over his arch-enemy Haman, it must have been bittersweet in the light of the edict' (2002: 61). The author is less reticent about Haman's feelings. He rushes home *with his head covered, in grief* (cf. 2 Sam. 15:30; Jer. 14:3–4). This act of self-humiliation partially mirrors Mordecai's putting on sackcloth and wailing (4:1), though Haman's action is more about the grief of shame than it is about the grief of loss (or, as in Mordecai's case, the potential for loss). In verse 8 Haman's head will be covered again, but this time he will have no say in the matter, as he is removed from public view. As Laniak puts it, Haman is beginning to 'disintegrate through the various steps of death' (1998: 120) and this is another stage in the shaming that culminates in his death.

13. Haman arrives home to blurt out *everything that had happened to him* (cf. the same phrase used of Mordecai's explanation to Hathach [4:7], but also note Haman's full account of the day's events in 5:11–13). It is perhaps a note of irony that this time his *friends* (5:14) are called *advisers* (lit. 'wise ones'). Their advice, which is constructed as a statement of fact, does not even have a hint of friendliness about it. It deals Haman a double blow, because it isolates him as the enemy of Mordecai (even his wife joins in) and suggests that his ruin is already in progress and he can do nothing about it. Their statement is both a gloomy prognosis for Haman and a reluctant recognition of the surviving quality of the Jewish people. It has been suggested that the confessional element here is in reality the author's view rather than that of Zeresh and the advisers (Bush 1996: 416–417, 420). However, as this narrator keeps his views very much to himself as the main story-line develops, it is equally probable that the words are based upon the lessons of history and accompanying superstitions. The Hebrew root *npl* ('to fall') occurs three times in this short statement and is an important motif in the story (see 3:7; 6:10; 7:8; 8:17; 9:2–3, 24). It signals here that the end has begun for Haman and 'with these words, the narrative foreshadows the culminating triumph – honour – of the Jews' (Klein 1995: 167).

14. The speed of events is emphasized by the phrase, *While they were still talking with him* (cf. Job 1:16–18), *the king's eunuchs arrived and hurried Haman away* (cf. vv. 10 and 12). Now Haman has no control over circumstances or coincidences, and he is summoned by eunuchs in just the same way as Vashti was before she disappeared from the royal court (cf. 1:10–11). As Haman arrives harassed, Esther assumes control.

ii. Esther's second banquet takes place (7:1–2)

These two verses mirror almost exactly the introduction to the first banquet of Esther (cf. 5:5b–6). It is significant that Esther is called *Queen Esther* (rather than just *Esther*, cf. 5:5b) in the light of the role she now assumes. Her plea to Xerxes will be made on the basis of her royal role. By the repetition of Xerxes' questions, tension and suspense are sustained as we wait to see if and how Esther will respond to him. Note that Esther crafts her response (v. 3) around the two questions Xerxes poses, which she has, of course, heard before. The impression is that Esther has planned her every move very carefully. Taking her cues from Xerxes, in this way she implies her attentive respect for him.

iii. Esther exposes Haman and his plot (7:3–6)

Now Esther's moment has arrived, she wastes no time. She treads a thin line because she needs to accuse Haman explicitly without implicating Xerxes. She does this by unveiling Haman as an enemy of Xerxes (and so takes up Mordecai's mantle [cf. 2:19–23]) and by employing skills of rhetoric and persuasion.

3. Esther's words are poetic and climactic. In the context of this cosy scene of wining and dining, their shock value must have been high! Esther passionately implores her king (*O king*), throwing herself on his mercy and *favour* and in so doing 'invoke(s) the honor of the one who called the relationship into being' (Laniak 1998: 114). For the first time, Esther fully reveals herself as Jewish and identifies herself with her people's plight. This is the moment when Mordecai's challenge to her (4:13–14) takes hold of her life.

4. One of the striking characteristics of Esther's reply to Xerxes is that in so few words she manages to say so much. She begins by picking up on the wording of the edict, repeating the same three words 'to destroy, to kill, to annihilate' from 3:13 (see NRSV, but note NIV changes the second verb from 'kill' to 'slaughter' which hides the parallelism). Bechtel (2002: 64) suggests that Esther uses the triplet here to ensure that Xerxes understands that he has not just passed an edict to enslave (*'bd*) the Jews but to destroy (*'bd*) them. Bechtel calls these verbs 'virtual homophones' and asks whether Xerxes was duped into believing that his edict legitimized the lesser of these two evils. What is certain is that by these words Esther indicates to Xerxes her awareness of the edict and her belief that this amounts to her people being *sold* (possibly a subtle indication that she knows Haman has bribed the king with money; see comments on 3:9 and 4:7). The rest of the verse is difficult to translate because some of the key words have more than one meaning. Esther claims she *would have kept quiet* if she and her people *had merely been sold as male and female slaves*, and that she would have taken this stance for the king's sake. The difficulty comes in deciding whether *ṣār* is a reference to the people's adversary (see NIV footnote) or to the adversity/trouble caused to the king by Esther's plea (see NIV text). The difficulties in translation are furthered by the word *nēzeq* which also has two meanings ('loss, financial loss' and 'trouble, annoyance'), and the uncertain meaning of the rare word *šōweh* ('to justify, to be commensurate with'; see also comments on 3:8 and Bush, 1996: 422). In light of the context of this phrase – it is part of Esther's impassioned plea – it is reasonable to wonder whether the imprecision of language and the double meanings here are intended features. It is as if Esther pours out one idea upon another; she uses words that would have rung bells in Xerxes' ears, suggesting injustice and crisis, indicating her apprehension and deference to the king, drawing on elements of the story she had heard. In so doing, Esther carefully aligns herself with the king's own interests.

5. Xerxes' response to Esther is introduced by the repetition of the verb 'to say' (lit. 'King Xerxes said and said to Queen Esther'). Although sometimes taken as a dittograph, a double appearance of this verb features in other OT passages (e.g. Gen. 22:7; 2 Sam. 24:17; Neh. 4:2 [MT, 3:34]; Ezek. 10:2), where it implies either solemnity or hesitation on the part of the speaker. Certainly, the drama of the verse is intensified if we allow both verbs to stand. The king asks, 'Who is he and where is he who dared to do this?' The questions are terse and have a derogatory ring. It is clear that Xerxes is putting distance between himself, the authority behind the edict, and the edict's designer and instigator.

6. Esther identifies Haman by what amounts to four synonyms. The TNIV conveys the abrupt nature of the text: 'An adversary and enemy! This vile Haman' (which improves the smoother reading of the NIV). Esther attacks Haman's role and character, and does not restrict his evil to his anti-Jewish stance. Again with economy of words she is casting him as her enemy (he has conspired against the queen's life), the king's enemy (she is Xerxes' wife and Haman has manipulated Xerxes), and the enemy of all people, by this string of words that accuse him of villainy.

This time the narrator leaves us in no doubt about Haman's response: he is literally *terrified*. The writer subtly indicates that a shift has occurred: it is no longer the king and Haman who drink wine together (cf. 3:15); now the queen stands with the king against his once-trusted servant and Haman is *terrified before them*. A change in relationships has occurred, which has put Esther where Haman once stood. There is also a subtle contrast with Mordecai: Haman is fearful in the presence of the king and Esther, whereas Mordecai showed no fear of Haman (see comments on 5:9). Haman's fear is induced, it seems, by the realization that Esther has given Xerxes no choice but to choose between herself and him. Haman reads the signs and senses the vibes against him.

B. Haman's death (7:7–10)

i. Xerxes' anger is roused (7:7–8)

7. The king (perhaps overwhelmed by the sheer number of dilemmas that face him) 'gets up in his anger' (lit.), leaves his wine and heads for the palace garden. Haman plays his final card and 'stays to seek his life' (lit.) from Queen Esther, 'for he saw that there was evil determined against him by the king' (NKJV). There is irony and pathos here: the tables have turned, Haman replaces Esther as the one who needs to 'request/beg' (compare the use of the verb *bqš* in 5:3, 6; 7:2) and he has to beg Esther, not even the king.

8. The end comes for Haman as the result of circumstances and coincidences conspiring against him in a farcical manner. Haman chooses to break court etiquette in a last attempt to save his life (see Yamauchi, 1990: 262, quoting an edict about conduct in the harem that directs that a courtier or eunuch 'when he would speak with a woman of the palace should not approach closer than seven steps'). Xerxes returns to the banquet hall to find Haman in a compromising position, and immediately jumps to conclusions and accuses Haman of attempting to molest the queen. Whether the author intends that Xerxes sees this as a good excuse to get rid of Haman without implicating himself, or whether he intends to stress that trust has totally broken down between Haman and Xerxes, Haman's action here is explained as an attempt to save his life rather than an attempt to assault Esther. So the final blow to Haman's life comes by way of a false accusation, not dissimilar to the injustice of false accusation that the Jewish people themselves have suffered at Haman's hands. Laniak (1998: 115) suggests that the whole incident is based around the king's concern for his own honour. This is what determines Haman's fate, and breaking court rules, especially in relation to the queen, is the final straw. By covering his face, Haman is removed from public view. The act of face covering may

imply guilt or shame (cf. Ps. 34:4 [MT, 34:5] and see comments on 6:12) and that Haman is a condemned man (being prepared for execution according to Greek and Roman custom). In addition, Haman is silenced just like Vashti (1:10ff.) and the Jews (3:6ff.) who suffered a similar injustice. He is given no opportunity to make a defence, as events speedily overtake him again; this happens 'as soon as the word left the king's mouth'. There is no indication of intervention by Esther to put the record straight about Haman's intentions. While this has sometimes been seen as a weakness in the narrator's portrayal of Esther as a heroine of integrity, it should be remembered that the removal of Haman was a prerequisite for Esther's larger mission – to save her people.

ii. Haman is put to death (7:9–10)

9–10. Events proceed as the reader might expect. Meeting Xerxes' need to make a decision, one of his seven eunuchs, Harbona (cf. 1:10), tells him about the extra high gallows Haman has constructed by his house, adding that Haman intended them for Mordecai (the man whom the king has recently honoured). Xerxes grabs this as an immediate solution to his problems (following his normal decision-making style, see Memucan's role in ch. 1 and Haman's in ch. 3). For the second time, Haman exchanges places with Mordecai, but whereas the first time was all about not receiving expected honour (ch. 6), now it is about receiving expected and ultimate shaming by being impaled on poles (see comments on 5:14). Again the irony of reversal is dramatic: Haman had intended that Xerxes should utter the final words of condemnation, 'impale him on it', but had intended that Mordecai should be the subject!

Xerxes' anger, not mentioned since verse 5, finally subsides now that Haman has been dealt with (cf. comments on 2:1). This brief description of the king's improved emotional state signifies a change of heart and mind, and prepares the reader for the lifting of tension in the subsequent chapters.

Meaning

Although the reversal of fortunes for Haman and Mordecai has been achieved, the crisis of the story has not yet been resolved.

There is still an edict out there that needs to be made null and void. With Haman's fall finally achieved, Esther can now re-emerge (she has been kept out of the story while Haman's death was secured). Esther re-emerges with her triumph over Haman inspiring her with confidence and the reader with hope. Mordecai can also re-emerge, because Haman's demise has not been a result of his personal vendetta against him, but has resulted from Haman's own evilness being uncovered. Haman has faced death and pleaded for life, but has now died. Esther's people are facing death and she has pleaded for their lives, but, despite flickers of hope, their future is still in the balance.

The last Persian banquet has taken place with Esther as host. The remaining banquets will celebrate Jewish honour and success. The resolution of the story is in view.

9. FULL SUCCESS: THE JEWISH PEOPLE ARE SAVED (Esther 8:1 – 9:16)

Context

The second part of Esther's mission, the saving of her people, assumes centre stage. Mordecai is central to this part of her mission. Together they have joint authority as the resolution of the story approaches. Chapters 8 and 9 adopt a matter-of-fact style (similar to that of chs. 1 and 2) and produce the political resolution of the crisis (in contrast to the personal aspects dealt with in ch. 7). Many features of the language, imagery and themes in chapters 8 and 9 find their basis in earlier sections of the story. Through careful symmetrical design the narrator comments on the story implicitly by presenting the events here as a reversal of previous ones. However, this is not an exact mirror image of what has gone before, as much goes beyond the expectations of exact reversal. Although the present reverses past events, it also supersedes it abundantly! The narrator's artistic skills become apparent, as previous episodes are inverted and intertwined in these last few chapters. The reader is, at one level, not challenged (because so much here has been seen before), but at the same time is required to reflect carefully on the significance of the subtleties of the text.

Comment

A. Mordecai and Esther find favour before Xerxes (8:1–4)

1. The chapter opens with two summary statements that indicate that a reversal has occurred whereby Esther and Mordecai became beneficiaries. Queen Esther (and she is only referred to by this formal title from here onwards) is given 'the house of Haman' (appropriately translated as *the estate of Haman*, cf. Gen. 39:4). There is varied evidence that the property of convicted criminals was at the disposal of the crown (see Herodotus 3:129; Josephus, *Antiquities* 11:17; Ezra 6:11). The reversal here means Haman's wealth (associated with his pride and evil plan) is passed to Queen Esther. Haman's demise is to her practical benefit, as it is also for Mordecai. He is now able to come *into the presence of the king* like the special men who had access to the king (see comments on 1:14) including Haman himself (see 3:8 and 5:11). So Mordecai replaces Haman, but his elevation is connected to Esther, *for Esther had told how he was related to her*. The Hebrew phrase is literally 'what he was to her' (see NKJV, NRSV), which potentially means more than just a family relationship. Mordecai has been Esther's wise adviser, faithful protector and the one who motivates, challenges and inspires her. Xerxes cannot afford to ignore these qualities now that Haman needs replacing. It seems as if Esther and Mordecai are now perceived as a single entity consisting of complementary qualities. In sum, Esther is saying to Xerxes, 'take us together'.

2. Esther 8:2–17 combines many aspects found in Esther 3:10 – 4:3. By removing the signet ring now *reclaimed from Haman* (cf. 3:10), the king signals another reversal. Haman abused the power embodied in the king's signet ring, but Xerxes sees no risk in handing over the ring again with Mordecai as the recipient. As Xerxes hands over his ring, Esther hands over the estate of Haman to Mordecai, making Esther both 'the cause and the agent of the reward Mordecai receives' (Fox 1991: 90).

In these two verses the honour play-acted in chapter 6 is actual-ized: Mordecai, this time with Esther at his side, has replaced and superseded Haman.

3. In contrast to the inflammatory audience with the king in the previous chapter, Esther now fulfils more closely the wish of Mordecai that she should *go into the king's presence to beg for mercy and plead with him*. The physical actions that accompany her plea (falling and weeping) add melodrama at a point where the reader might already think the crisis is over. They also portray Esther as someone who intercedes humbly on behalf of her people. The narrator explains that Esther identified the plan against the Jews as being devised by *Haman the Agagite* (cf. comments on 3:1), making no reference to Xerxes' role. The emphasis lies upon Haman's ill inten-tions and deliberate planning (cf. Jer. 11:19 and Dan. 11:25). Esther asks the king to 'revoke' (lit. 'pass over/reverse') the evil of Haman and his plot. The negative tone cannot be missed.

4. The gold sceptre signals that Esther finds favour with the king (cf. 5:2). He encourages her to rise in his presence. This second mention of the sceptre is a timely reminder that Esther still performs a precarious role, but now there is little tension because we know Xerxes is favourably disposed towards her. This has already been established, and Esther can play to this knowledge as she takes up the challenge to deal with the outstanding matter of the edict of destruction. The irony is that the king has given Esther material things to indicate his favour, but her central concern has not yet been addressed.

B. The issue of overturning Haman's edict is addressed (8:5–14)

i. Esther asks for a new edict (8:5–6)

5. Esther's opening words pile on the flattery in a way that goes beyond her previous attempts (cf. 5:4, 7–8; 7:3). The four indi-vidual phrases perhaps indicate her own awareness that she is about to ask for the almost impossible! The new phrase here is *if he … thinks it the right thing to do*, which shows deference to the king's opinion in a way, incidentally, that Haman has never done. Esther dares to add *and if he is pleased **with me*** (not '**with it**' i.e. my idea), providing contrast to other occurrences of this phrase in the story (e.g. 1:19; 3:9). Esther's confidence is based in Xerxes' respect for her.

Esther refers to Haman's edict by the term 'dispatches' (NRSV 'letters'), which means that the irrevocable overtones attached to the word *dāt* ('law') are avoided. She also describes Haman in terms associated with his most evil moment (3:1), reminding the king that *the Jews in all the king's provinces* are facing destruction. Her request amounts to 'let it be written to overrule/annul' Haman's dispatches. The verb is *šûb* ('to turn around', here in a form meaning 'to turn back, to revoke'; cf. Judg. 11:35 where it is used of a vow that cannot be broken). The choice of verb matches Esther's description of Haman's edict as 'dispatches' − if she had called that 'law' then the verb *'br* ('to pass over') would be expected (see comments on 1:9).

6. Esther's personal agony is emphasized by adding this rhetorical question to her request. The rhetoric amounts to Esther claiming that it is impossible for her to survive the pain of seeing disaster come upon her people (cf. Song 5:3). Esther has identified herself with the Jewish people by taking up their cause; now she identifies herself with them emotionally (as Mordecai had done, 4:1).

ii. Xerxes hands the matter over to Esther and Mordecai (8:7–8)

7–8. Xerxes now addresses Esther and Mordecai together, suggesting that he now sees them as they see themselves (see vv. 1–2). Xerxes' tone is 'sharp and exasperated' (Bush 1996: 445), although this is hidden in the NIV because the two words indicating such emotion (*hinnēh*, 'behold/look', v. 7, and *'attem*, emphatic 'you', v. 8) are not translated (contrast NRSV). Xerxes' own emphasis seems to be, 'Now look here I have given … You, you write about the Jews as you like.' This reaction is consistent with what we expect from an impetuous king, who doesn't like responsibility and would rather delegate to someone else when his quick and easy response to a crisis is not received as a solution. Maybe the irony is not lost on Xerxes: is he impotent, bound by his own laws and therefore less powerful to achieve what he wants than is the dead man Haman?

Meaning

The echoes of 3:10–11 are obvious: Esther and Mordecai are told to do as they please just as Haman was, and to use the signet ring to achieve it. Just as Haman was given permission to become the enemy of the people and the story's villain, Esther and Mordecai are given permission to secure their deliverance and become the story's heroes. The king does not offer advice about how they can annul Haman's edict, but he (or possibly the narrator) adds a timely reminder that revoking what has been written is not a simple matter. What can Esther and Mordecai devise to counteract what has gone before?

iii. Mordecai oversees the writing of a new edict (8:9–10)

Context

Esther 8:9–12 mirrors 3:12–15 (see below). The section explains that a second edict was written and distributed in the same way as the edict of Haman, but with the clear purpose of reversing its effects. The differences between the two passages reflect the changed circumstances. The administrative strength of the Persian communication system is now utilized by Jews for Jews with the same sort of haste, efficiency and urgency that was applied to Haman's edict.

Comment

   9. This time it is *Mordecai's orders* rather than *Haman's* that are written out (3:12), and *the Jews* are listed as the first recipients. This edict is applicable to all the people of all the 127 provinces (see comments on 1:1 and 1:22), and each receive the edict in their own *script and language*. By adding *and also to the Jews in their script and language*, there is an important deviation from the parallel verses in 3:12–15. Whereas Haman had no concern for Jewish interests, now Jewish interests are central. This phrase also adds dignity to the Jewish people, for language is 'a sign of ethnic vitality and power' (Berlin 2001: 76). Mordecai's edict is written on the twenty-third day of the third month, Sivan (cf. Haman's edict written on the thirteenth day of the first month), implying that the events since chapter 3 have taken place in the intervening two months and ten

days. There is nothing to suggest that this is an unlikely framework, although the Greek versions schedule both edicts in the first month, suggesting that the intervening events took place over a ten-day period.

10a. Mordecai seals the edict with the king's signet ring, signifying the reality that authority has passed from Haman to Mordecai. In these administrative matters Queen Esther is left on the sidelines. Her task had been to implore the king for mercy: Mordecai is quite capable of seeing through the necessary arrangements.

iv. The new edict is distributed (8:10 –14)

10b. The terms describing the types of horses used to distribute the edict are difficult to translate into English (in fact, the Hebrew writer has just transliterated Persian terms into Hebrew characters). Together they imply that the very best royal-bred horses were used to ensure the express delivery of this new edict. So the descriptions associated with this second edict supersede those relating to the first; hence Mordecai's edict (and its author) is elevated as superior.

11–12. Verse 11 summarizes what the edict permitted. It enabled Jews to 'assemble and protect themselves' (TNIV, lit. 'to stand up for themselves'), terms used for positioning an army to defend against an attack. The rest of the verse has been variously translated, especially by those trying to avoid the meaning that the Jews killed and plundered men, women and children. However, by appreciating the literary design of the story, and the importance of reversal to its structure, the meaning of this summary of the edict's instructions can be understood. The verbs *to destroy, kill and annihilate* are lifted from Haman's edict (see 3:13). The next phrase also mirrors the description of Haman's edict except for the fact that *all the Jews* (3:13) becomes *any armed force* (8:11). 'Children and women, and to plunder their goods' (NRSV, 8:11) is also lifted from 3:13 (with slight changes in word order). Similarly in verse 12, 'on one day' is taken from 3:13, along with the identification of the date (the thirteenth of Adar) and the phrase 'in every province of the king'. Each phrase in 8:13 is also found in 3:13, with the exception of the final phrase *to avenge themselves on their enemies*. The author is obviously concerned to show that this edict permits an exact reversal of the

Jews' fortunes. Mordecai's edict reverses Haman's edict by giving power to those from whom all power had been removed. It is this point that is primary and that dominates the author's description of the new edict. He chooses to extract sections from chapter 3 that make this reversal clear because this is consistent with his story's design and purpose. The moral issues are not meant to detain the reader, although some are addressed at a later point (e.g. only men are mentioned in the head count of the dead and the Jews did not take plunder [see comments on 9: 6, 16] and the attack is limited to one day).

So the text needs to be interpreted as it stands, rather than be watered down to accommodate modern moral standards. This is justifiable in the first instance, as has been demonstrated by the literary parallelism within this story, but there are also important theological grounds for maintaining the force of the text as it stands. After all, Haman the Amalekite represents all enemies of the Jews (see comments on 3:1). By destroying the enemies of God, the Jews in Persia complete the task that Saul in Israel left unfinished. For Jewish readers the parallelism with Saul's attack against the Amalekites would not be missed, especially the specific instruction Saul received to totally destroy them, *men, women, children and infants* … (1 Sam. 15:3). The edict of Mordecai is therefore a means by which the evil intent of Haman, and all the enmity in history he represents, is resolved and reversed in favour of the Jews.

13. The phrase *to avenge themselves on their enemies* is the only new element in the verse and interprets the action of the Jews as a form of vengeance. Berlin suggests that the verb used (*nqm*) means 'not senseless killing but justified retaliation' (2001: 78). Followed by the particle *min* ('from'), as is the case here, this seems an appropriate interpretation (cf. the verb plus particle in Judg. 16:28 and 1 Sam. 14:24 where Samson and Saul seek vengeance against the Philistines).

14. This verse mirrors Esther 3:15, except it does not mention the Jews sitting down and relaxing as Haman and Xerxes had done. Note that the speed of this edict's distribution supersedes the previous description: the couriers here *raced out* (i.e. 'made urgent haste' rather than just 'haste', 3:15).

Meaning
This passage mirrors and supersedes the parallel passage in Esther 3. It points to the reversal that has taken place and anticipates its further demonstration in the verses that follow.

C. The Jews' mourning is replaced by joy (8:15–17)

Context
Verses 15–17 intertwine previous sections of the story. They draw on aspects of 3:14–15 (highlighting Mordecai's role as Haman's successor); they use descriptive elements from chapter 1 (especially v. 6, emphasizing Mordecai's royal honour); and, through reminiscences of chapter 6 (especially vv. 6–11), they indicate that the enacted honour Mordecai received is now actualized. The irony works at a number of different levels, but the emphasis is that the honour Mordecai receives goes beyond that which Haman ever achieved. Fortunes have been reversed, but the outcome supersedes reversal expectations.

Comment

i. Mordecai's honour is complete (8:15)
The description of Mordecai's present garb contrasts with the sackcloth and ashes described in 4:1. There Mordecai's clothing was accompanied by his own wailing and also that of the Jews (see comments on 4:1). Here the city of Susa is united again, the Jews are not distinguished from the other inhabitants, and this time the mood is *joyous celebration.*

ii. The Jews' gladness is complete (8:16–17)
The four words 'happiness', 'joy', 'gladness', 'honour' (v. 16) are the antitheses of the four words 'mourning', 'fasting', 'weeping' and 'wailing' in 4:3. In fact, the word *'ôr* (translated *happiness*) means 'light', which can be used as a symbol of joy and 'participates in the semantic field of honor (i.e. "glory"; Isa. 58:8; 60:1, 19)' (Laniak 1998: 133, fn. 18). Laniak suggests that honour is confirmed by these words that denote public acclaim (1998: 132): by the people's response Mordecai and the Jews experience the removal

of their shame and the reinstatement of honour.

Verse 17 emphasizes that celebration pervaded every province and *city* (cf. 4:3 where only 'province' is mentioned). The meaning of the final sentence is unclear. First, the meaning of the phrase *many people of other nationalities became Jews* is not clear. The subject is 'people of the land' (i.e. non-Jews) and 'became Jews' might equally be translated 'professed to be Jews' (see Bush 1996: 436). This translation is helpful because it can carry the various ideas associated with the term, including pretending to be Jews and identifying with Jews. (There seems to be no justification for the addition in the Septuagint 'and were circumcised', which limits the understanding of this phrase to a cultic one.) Of importance is the parallel that this phrase creates with Esther's own journey: she chose to identify herself with her people despite the risks involved; now non-Jews choose to identify themselves with Jews because they see only benefits from doing so. The second issue concerns the nature of the fear that has gripped non-Jews. It could conceivably mean that the growing influence and power of the Jews are recognized now Mordecai is second in command. But this seems unlikely in the light of Mordecai's good reception in the city of Susa (see v. 15). It seems more consistent with the writer's use of previous elements in the story that the fear is related to the fulfilment of the words uttered by Zeresh (see comments on 6:13). Experience suggests that an inevitable victory is on its way: the Jews are now regarded with awe and respect just like Mordecai is himself. In addition, Laniak suggests that 'this type of fear describes a public perception of divine involvement; it reflects awe and colloquially, a "healthy respect"' (1998: 133).

Meaning
The dramatic tension is resolved, although the story's outcome has not yet been reached. Victory for the Jews seems secure, even assumed, but, like the pattern associated with Mordecai's honour (cf. chs. 6 and 8), Jewish victory over their enemies still needs to be confirmed on the appointed day – the thirteenth of Adar.

D. The enemies of the Jews are destroyed (9:1–16)

Context
Nine months after the events of the previous chapter, the appointed and long-anticipated day arrives, enabling victory to be secured.

Comment

i. 'Now the tables were turned' (9:1–5)

1. The double occurrence of 'day' emphasizes its importance and hints at the resolution of the story that has been expected but not yet experienced. The resolution is summarized as 'an overturning' (NIV *the tables were turned*). The Hebrew verb is *hpk* ('to overturn') and is emphatic here. It implies a complete turnaround of fortunes (such as when a curse becomes a blessing, see Deut. 23:5 and Neh. 13:2). It occurs with similar overtones in 9:22, where sorrow is 'overturned' to joy (cf. Ps. 30:11; Lam. 5:15; Isa. 61:3). The verb conveys changed circumstances and accompanying changed emotions. There are two appearances of the verb *šlṭ* ('to rule over'), though this is not easily seen in the NIV.[1] This verb explains the nature of the complete turnaround, whereby the 'overpowered/ruled over ones' become the 'overpowering/ruling over ones'. This is the author's summary of the change of fortunes that has taken place. He avoids referring to bloodthirsty victory, but uses terms that are associated with status and honour. The Jews' power is exercised against *those who hated them*; they now rule over those who, following Haman, wanted to strip them of all dignity and honour.

2. The appointed day is characterized by bold Jewish action (assembling for battle against their attackers, cf. 8:11) and a paralysing fear among other people (cf. 8:17). In their inability to stand before the Jews, the non-Jews as a whole now experience what Zeresh had predicted for Haman in particular (see 6:13).

3–4. Mordecai is at the centre of these verses that conclude the

---

1. NIV translates 'to overpower' and 'got the upper hand over'. Cf. RSV and NRSV that translate both occurrences of the verb in the same way ('to get mastery over' and 'to gain power over' respectively).

story. His personal fortunes are indicative of his people's fortunes. He, like them, has assumed power, earned a reputation and is feared. He is feared by all ranks of people, without any need for a king's command to order it (contrast Haman in 3:1–2). Previously Mordecai has only been labelled 'the Jew' (e.g. 6:10), but verse 4 ends with the phrase 'For the man Mordecai became more and more great' (lit., see NKJV that retains this emphasis). This construction is used in Exodus 11:3 in reference to Moses being highly regarded by the Egyptians. The description of Mordecai's honour here anticipates the statement with which the book ends in 10:2–3.

5. Although Mordecai's rise is part of the story's ending, verse 5 returns to the corporate victory of the Jews over *their enemies* and *those who hated them* (cf. the use of the same phrase at the end of v. 1). These phrases limit the Jewish action to retaliation and self-defence, even though the Jews have the freedom to 'do as they like' (cf. use of the same word in 1:8). The language used to describe the victory is compact and familiar (drawing on two of the three verbs associated with previous edicts, 3:13; 8:11).

Meaning

Together these five verses conclude the story by consolidating its resolution as an example of tables being turned. Details of the scale and means of victory are sparse because that might well detract from the reversal motif. What follows focuses on the outcome of the story and its effect on subsequent Jewish religion and history.

ii. The extent of the Jewish victory in Susa (9:6–12a)

Context

Rather than continuing in general overview terms, the author explains how the Jewish victory in Susa differed from the schedule of events in the provinces (cf. 9:6–12a and 9:12b–13). This in turn serves as the basis of the institution of Purim.

Comment

6. In the citadel of Susa (see comments on 1:2) 500 men are killed. It is much more likely that this is a round figure rather than an accurate head count (and is possibly a further example of exaggeration). What is more important is the fact that only men are counted: there is no reference to women and children being killed (see comments on 8:11).

7–10. Selected for special mention are the ten sons of Haman. Previous lists of names have added a comical quality to the text (see 1:10, 14), but here the layout of the Hebrew text is different, adding solemnity to the list. Each name stands alone, separated from the next by a line space and the sign of the direct object (cf. similar layout in Josh. 12:9–24). It is as if the author wants the reader to ponder each name, for with each death comes the final blow to Haman's pride (see 5:11) and all the enmity that history had nurtured (see comments on 3:1). The names themselves are Persian and are spelt with variation in the versions.

The significant phrase *but they did not lay hands on the plunder* occurs here for the first time and then punctuates the text (vv. 15 and 16). This is unexpected because the edict allowed such taking of booty (cf. 8:11). Whether this deliberately establishes the Jews here as morally superior to those who had taken a different path (cf. 1 Sam. 15:17–23) is disputable, but it clearly reiterates that the horrors of enmity have been halted.

11–12a. These verses repeat information the reader already knows (see v. 6), but clarifies that there is no delay in informing the king of the deaths in Susa. He was told *that same day*. It seems that the king is impressed by the figures quoted, which is ironic as there has been so much bloodshed in the royal city. Xerxes' question *What have they done in the rest of the king's provinces?* is rhetorical: he doesn't seem to expect an answer. However, the words are important, because the king voices the differentiation between the events in Susa and those elsewhere, preparing the way for the variations in Purim celebrations.

iii. Esther's further request on behalf of the Jews in Susa (9:12b–13)

12b. Although Xerxes' offer to Esther seems familiar, there are two noticeable differences from previous occurrences of Xerxes' benevolence. First, there is no indication that Esther intended to ask for anything; second, Xerxes doesn't offer her up to half his kingdom (cf. 5:2–3, 6; 7:1–2). Maybe Xerxes' inquiry is ironic, ('surely in the light of what has been achieved you can't want anything else'), or congratulatory ('you have done so well you deserve whatever else you desire'). The effect of the offer is important: it allows Esther to secure an extension to the edict's application in Susa.

13. Now more confident before the king, Esther shows less deference (cf. her words in 5:8; 7:3). She asks for two things: to continue to apply the edict for a further day in Susa, and for Haman's sons to be hanged on gallows. In the light of Esther's heroine status within the story, it is probably more in line with the author's intentions that Esther's request is read in a positive rather than a negative way. Rather than being indicative of her blood-thirsty nature, it is more likely that the reader should notice Esther's determination to eliminate hatred against the Jews. She doesn't ask for a new edict, nor for licence to do as she pleases. Instead, she operates within the confines of the edict Mordecai has already designed, focusing on the remaining opposition in Susa. By hanging the bodies of Haman's sons, Esther will resolve the remaining tension in the story: Haman's body has been disgraced, but now the line of enmity against the Jews is also permanently disgraced. This is the final act of victory over their enemies.

iv. Esther's request is granted (9:14–15)

14–15. Without any hesitation the king acquiesces and Esther's wishes are granted. The result is reported without emotion: on the day after the edict's appointed day the Jews assembled, killed 300 men and left the plunder untouched (see comments on v. 10). The brevity of the reporting style, together with the spotlight upon time scheduling, suggests that interest is now focused on the legacy of the story rather than the specifics of its outcome. The drama has already happened: its importance now relates to its impact on the future.

v. The extent of the Jewish victory in the provinces (9:16)

The answer to Xerxes' rhetorical question in verse 12 is revealed: in the provinces 75,000 (LXX 15,000) people are killed, not gratu-itously, but because the Jews needed relief/rest from their enemies (see comments on 4:14). Again the Jews do not take advantage of the situation by lifting the plunder (cf. vv. 10 and 15).

Meaning

Esther 8:1 – 9:16 provides the resolution of the story: the crisis faced by the Jews is turned over to their relief, benefit and joy. It also provides a link between the conclusion (victory) and outcome (the festival of Purim, 9:17–32). The theme of joy is a vital motif describing the emotions associated with both the conclusion and outcome (see end of ch. 8 and 9:17–32). It is because the anticipation and experience of victory resulted in joy that the story is remembered for ever in a joyous festival. Life for the Jewish people is changed for ever because they now have a new experience of victory, the memory of which they desire to perpetuate.

10. THE JEWS CELEBRATE THEIR VICTORY
(Esther 9:17–32)

Context

Esther 9:17–32 explains the outcome of the story: the celebration of the festival of Purim. The writer takes us out of the historical context of Esther and the Persian court into his own context, presumably some years later. He seems eager to explain the background, importance and priorities of the Purim festival that has emerged. The style and meaning of the text changes because it is now 'not narrational but legislative in purpose' (Bush 1996: 487).

The author advocates the acceptance of the festival of Purim and explains how it should be celebrated. The resulting text is a little unwieldy, lacking the order and clarity of the earlier narrative, but the writer is unperturbed by this because he brings together various elements that are inter-related in order to confirm Purim.

Although the status of verses 20–32 has been disputed (e.g. Clines labels them 'documentary appendices' [1984: 162]), various themes link these verses to the story that precedes them (e.g. rest, joy, honour, writing and feasting). So these themes assume importance in the Purim festivities and therefore in all future history of the Jews.

Comment

A. Spontaneous days of feasting (9:17–19)

These verses confirm that the Purim festival began as a spontaneous response from the Jewish community to the deliverance experienced in Esther's time.

17–19. Although verse 17 is connected to verse 16 (identifying the timing of the events in v. 16), the end of verse 17 mirrors the end of verse 18 and creates a parallel that is reiterated in verse 19. All three verses emphasize that in response to victory a day of rest was held that became *a day of feasting and joy.* (NB v. 19 adds *a day for giving presents to each other*). There is no regulating of the celebrations here, just recognition that a different schedule emerged in Susa from elsewhere. It is possible that the giving of gifts was originally associated with the provinces (see v. 19), although Mordecai's letters containing the gift-sending instructions were sent to *all the Jews* (v. 20). The record here means that the first ever celebration of the outcome of Esther's story was held in the provinces on the fourteenth of Adar. The second celebration took place on the fifteenth of Adar in Susa.

The emphasis on rest seems significant, because at other points in Jewish history the purpose of victory was connected to the relief that followed rather than to the honour of victory itself (see for example, Deut. 3:20; 12:9–10; Josh. 1:13, 15). In these other contexts, Yahweh is identified as the giver of rest to his people, and, although this religious interpretation is omitted in Esther, it is seemingly implied by the people's cultic response. As they are 'given' rest, so they 'give' gifts to each other. The word *mānôt* (NIV *presents*) means 'portions' (cf. RSV 'choice portions' or 'food portions'; NRSV 'gifts of food'; TNIV 'presents of food'; see also Dan. 1:5, 10) and has already appeared in 2:9. Sending gifts on occasions of celebration and joy is also mentioned in Nehemiah 8:10–12, where the people are encouraged to send gifts as part of their journey from grief to joy. This provides a parallel to the emotional journey the people of

God have experienced in the Esther story. It seems that sending gifts not only expresses joy but distributes and increases it, for it has communal as well as personal dimensions (see v. 22).

B. Mordecai himself confirms the festival (9:20–22)

Mordecai himself sends letters to commend the celebration of the rest achieved. The report of Mordecai's letters implies that only spontaneous celebration has occurred thus far, possibly indicating that Mordecai wrote to commend the celebrations after the initial spontaneity, but before the first anniversary of the event.

20. The phrase *Mordecai recorded these events* (lit. 'Mordecai wrote down these things') may indicate that Mordecai was himself the writer of the book of Esther, but it is more likely that it refers to Mordecai recording the spontaneous celebrations (9:17–19), which in turn formed the basis of the appeal in his letters. It is also possible that the phrase refers to the summary of the story (see comments on vv. 23–26).

21. The intention of Mordecai's letters is *to have them celebrate annually*. The same emphasis appears in verses 27 and 31, implying that the Jews made their own decision to celebrate Purim (cf. RSV 'enjoining themselves'). So Mordecai does not command the Jews to celebrate, but instead he encourages them to formalize the celebrations that had been spontaneously started. The reversal motif is again present: the Jews now make decisions rather than being merely subject to them as they were at the start of the story. The cultic life of the Jewish community is truly designed and owned by the community itself.

It is possible that the verse intends to establish uniformity in Judaism (both days celebrated by all Jews annually), but in the light of the fact that Jewish practice today still differs between the fourteenth and fifteenth of Adar, it appears that this was not the received meaning.

22. The reason for the celebration Mordecai commends is important. It is a celebration of the *relief* (or 'rest', see also vv. 17 and 18) and commemorates the month of reversal. By this emphasis, the Purim festival is stripped of military overtones and the idea of vengeance on enemies. Instead, it is more closely associated with the positive concepts of enjoying rest and expressing community, joy and gratitude. Mordecai urges the Jewish community to celebrate the anniversary of this great moment just as the Jews who experienced the deliverance at first hand had done. The addition of the phrase *and gifts to the poor* may indicate a supplementary requirement, or it may serve to explain that the gifts mentioned in verse 19 included this expression of social concern.

C. The festival of Purim is established (9:23–32)

i. A summary of the festival's historical roots (9:23–26a)

23. This verse confirms that Mordecai's letters met with success, in that the Jews *agreed to continue the celebration they had begun*. Its essence is repeated in verse 27 (see comments below), and together these verses form an *inclusio* around the summary of the story that comes in the intervening verses.

24–25. On the basis of verse 26 it is probable that this short summary of the Esther narrative formed part of the content of either the letters mentioned in verse 20 or a subsequent letter from Mordecai. In the summary Esther and Mordecai play no part; Haman is the evil protagonist and King Xerxes saves the day by giving *written orders* to secure the end of Haman's plans. There is no mention of the Jewish military victory on the thirteenth and fourteenth of Adar. The prominence given to the *pûr*, mentioned last in 3:7, also serves to centralize Haman and his evil plot, and emphasizes that a reversal has occurred (for the day determined for destruction has become a reason for joy and a prelude to rest). As Fox explains, this summary is not identical to the story's narrative form because 'it presents the story from a different perspective … [it is] a paraphrastic extraction from Mordecai's epistle' (1991: 120). Clines suggests it represents a Persian view of events (1990: 49).

26a. The explanation of the festival's name gives only the barest summary of the reasons for this label. Simply put, because *pûr* occurred in the story, it was adopted (in a plural form consistent with other festivals, e.g. weeks, tabernacles, lights) as a suitable name for the commemorative festival. Perhaps this name itself was deliberately intended to move the focus of the commemoration from military victory to overcoming evil. Alternatively, it may infer that the religious meaning of the story includes the idea that the fate of God's people is not decided by evil men throwing die, but by God alone who assigns to his people their portion (see Ps. 16:5–6).

ii. A summary of the commitment of the Jews to this festival (9:26b–28)

26b. The perpetual celebration is accepted by the Jewish community as an apt response to this letter and to what they themselves have seen and experienced.

27–28. The community *took it upon themselves* to decide that this annual celebration should be held by all Jews now and in the future, and also by *all who join them* (see comments on 8:17). The emphasis is clearly on all-inclusiveness, and the language mirrors the style in earlier sections of the narrative (cf. 1:22; 3:14; 8:9, 13).

In verse 28, the Hebrew verb 'to remember' (*zkr*) is used twice. This verb is commonly connected with cultic activity (cf. the instruction to commemorate the exodus so that its memory may not fade in Exod. 13). Festivals serve to remind one generation of what they have seen and experienced, but they also perpetuate the memory for those who were not first-hand witnesses of deliverance.

In the Jewish calendar today, the Sabbath preceding Purim is called *Shabbot Zachor* (the Sabbath of remembering). On this Sabbath the readings are Exodus 17:8–16 (the instruction to Moses to write down what Joshua needs to remember, i.e. that God will wipe out the memory of Amalek) and Deuteronomy 25:17–19 (the instruction to Israel to remember what the Amalekites did, not forgetting that God will give them rest from their enemies so the memory of the Amalekites will be wiped out). Far from distracting from the story, these verses aid our appreciation of its meaning and historical significance.

iii. Esther confirms the festival (9:29–32)

Although the preceding verses bring the narrative to a good conclusion, another layer of support for the festival is cited. Esther herself re-enters the text and stands alongside Mordecai, undertaking the tasks of writing, confirming, decreeing and establishing.

Mordecai is normally identified as the masculine singular subject of the verb 'and he sent' (see v. 30, NIV, TNIV), even though his name does not appear in this verse. According to this reading, Mordecai is involved in the task of propagating Esther's letters. If the verb is treated as impersonal ('Letters were sent', see RSV, NRSV) – even though the passive impersonal would normally require a plural verb – then Mordecai is not involved. Both interpretations are possible on account of the difficult construction. The writer's primary concern here lies with establishing Esther's support for the perpetual celebration of the festival, and this perhaps explains the rather sketchy and hurried information relating to the letters' circulation. Esther writes *with full authority* (i.e. she uses all her authority as queen to confirm Purim). The words of the letters sent to the provinces are described as 'words of peace and truth' (lit. NIV *words of good will and assurance*; cf. the similar words in Zech. 8:19), which suggests at least that they were benevolent in character even if instructive in content.

The mention of fasting in verse 31 is perhaps unexpected, but recalls the fasts previously mentioned in 4:3 and 4:16. It seems that 9:31 might well be an encouragement to the Jewish people to see the new festival as a final reversal of all the weeping and wailing which their times of fasting had represented.

So verse 32 establishes Esther as the final authority in the establishment of Purim. It is to be a festival for ever because her story is a story for ever, and for that reason it is written down and immortalized. The narrative has shown that it is when events and laws are written down that they become indisputable and permanent.

Meaning

This confirmation and legitimization of the Purim festival, with its multiple layers, may bear evidence to the obstacles that were faced when the importance of this non-Torah festival was impressed upon the Jewish community. It also bears witness to several principles that underpin the Jewish faith, including that it is a historically based faith in which practice emerges from experiences, and experiences are remembered, written down and celebrated. History is important to the Jews because history is the journey of God with his people, whether God seems abundantly present or apparently absent. The recorder of these evidences of Purim's legitimization commends the processes by which elements in Jewish history and practice are confirmed and re-affirmed by both the response and decision of community and the commendation of key players in its history. But these verses also affirm that history itself finds value when it shapes and defines the present. By the establishment of the Purim festival for all generations, the story of Esther is credited as significant and effective not only in its original historical setting, but also for all Jewish communities for all time to come. In this sense, Purim itself legitimizes the writing down of the Esther story: its message will live on.

Additional note: Purim today

The festival of Purim is still celebrated in Jewish communities today. The festival celebrates the inviolability of the Jewish people due to God's decisive acts of deliverance for their sake, and it provides a religious framework for the interpretation of the events of the story.

The Purim festival has become a Purim season that begins with the *Shabbat Shekalim* (the Sabbath of Shekels) that occurs on the Sabbath before the beginning of the month of Adar. The readings on this Sabbath commend the giving of money (shekels).

The Sabbath immediately before the fourteenth of Adar is called the *Shabbat Zachor* (the Sabbath of Remembrance, see notes above on 9:27–28) when the history of the enmity between Jews and Amalekites is recalled.

On the thirteenth of Adar, the Jews fast as they remember the risk Esther took on behalf of her people. The requirements on this solemn day include abstention from eating, drinking, wearing of leather shoes, washing and engaging in sexual activity. At the conclusion of the fast (on the eve of Purim), the book of Esther is read out in its entirety, preceded by the pronouncement of three blessings that praise God for his miraculous deeds. The concluding blessing reads:

> Blessed are you Lord our God, King of the universe,
> who has contended for us and defended our cause,

avenging us by bringing retribution on all our mortal enemies and
   delivering us from our adversaries.
Blessed are You, Lord, who delivers His people from all their adversaries –
   God who saves.

On the morning of Purim the Esther scroll is read again in the synagogue, but the mood is lighter. In fact, children dress up as the main characters in the story, and the carnival atmosphere is enhanced by the telling of jokes and the singing of songs. When Haman's name is mentioned, children make a loud noise using various home-made shakers. Two types of gifts are sent: food parcels to friends and family, and charitable donations for the poor. Towards the end of the day, Jewish families gather together for a relaxed meal. Today it is only the Jews in Jerusalem (a walled city) who celebrate Purim on the fifteenth day of Adar – all other Jews celebrate on the fourteenth of Adar.[1]

So the Purim celebrations today follow the events and procedures laid out in the book of Esther, providing a theological framework for its interpretation. The festival is thus a vivid reminder that unexpected reversals do happen in history, and such reversals have a permanent impact on the life of the community of faith who celebrate the powerful presence of God among them.

----

1. This information has been extracted from an article by Amy J. Kramer, entitled 'Purim: Law and Customs' (*Everything Jewish*, 1998–99).

11. CONCLUSION: MORDECAI'S HONOUR: 'He worked for the good of his people' (Esther 10:1–3)

Context

After the aetiological interlude about Purim, chapter 10 marks a return to narrative concerns. These three verses balance the introduction to the Esther story in 1:1–9. Just as the opening verses of chapter 1 take the original readers into Esther's world, the final verses take the intended readers out of that world to reflect from their perspective on the legacy of the story. Berlin (2001: 94) suggests that chapter 10 is a 'coda' that 'serves an important narrative function', and certainly it seems to conclude the Hebrew scroll satisfactorily. But it also serves a didactic purpose, for it gives value to the narrative as a story of consequence to its readers past, present and future.

Comment

1. Although it is surprising that the opening verse of this 'coda' is concerned with the fact that *King Xerxes imposed tribute throughout the empire*, it is probably more significant than it seems. First, this

verse parallels 1:1 by emphasizing the vastness of the king's realm, but this time the text goes even further. It uses a phrase to describe the extent of his rule (lit. 'the land and the coastlands of the sea', see NRSV and NKJV) that signifies the whole known inhabited earth (cf. Isa. 42:4 and 10 where the same words are used for the extent of the servant's rule and the sources of the Lord's praise). So it seems that by the end of the story, Xerxes' rule was even more secure: his power and honour have increased. Secondly, this phrase also indicates that normality has returned in the Persian Empire. The story has seen Xerxes tempted to gain wealth through acquiescing to Haman's evil intent (see comments on 3:9–11), but now he has reverted to the more acceptable means of government. (*Tribute* [NIV] is actually the translation of the word *mas,* which elsewhere in the OT is used to mean forced labour. It is generally agreed that by this point in history it has assumed the meaning of monetary tribute or taxation.) So life in the Persian Empire has settled down again. But it seems that things are no longer the same for Xerxes: instead things are better! Like the promoted Joseph before him, the promoted Mordecai has brought better times for the one who recognized his talents and secured his promotion (cf. Gen. 47:26).

2. Xerxes' reign is summarized by this statement, which is modelled on rhetorical questions that often conclude narratives about the lives of the kings of Judah (see e.g. 1 Kgs 11:41; 14:29; 15:23; 16:14; 2 Chr. 25:26). The writer claims authority for his record of events by referring to the written records about the kings of Media and Persia that verify Xerxes' *acts of power and might,* including his elevation of Mordecai. The verb *gdl* ('to be great') is used twice in this verse (and once in v. 10) in relation to Mordecai. Although Xerxes promoted him to a place of greatness, this term, so closely associated with Xerxes in the prologue (see 1:4), and then later referring to Haman (see 3:1; 5:11), is used in 9:4, and repeatedly here in the coda of Mordecai himself. As the coda reflects the rhetoric of the OT texts that record the deaths of the kings of Judah, it is conceivable that verses 2 and 3 should be understood as epitaphs. The first in verse 2 relates to the king (as custom dictated), but beginning in verse 2 and completed in verse 3 an epitaph for Mordecai's own life emerges.

3. Verse 3 contrasts Mordecai with Haman. Haman was once given *a seat of honour higher than that of all the other nobles* (3:1), but now that the great reversal has taken place, it is Mordecai who is remembered as *second in rank to King Xerxes*. Haman has been presented as a self-centred and self-indulgent man, but Mordecai is remembered as someone who spoke and worked for the good of others. Mordecai is remembered as *pre-eminent among the Jews* and as being *held in high esteem by his many fellow Jews*, whereas Haman had earned himself the title 'enemy of the Jews'. Haman's life was committed to the task of evil and destruction; Mordecai's life was directed towards goodness (*ṭôb*) and peace (*šālôm*, NIV *welfare*).

This verse offers an interesting comment on 7:9, where one of the king's eunuchs describes Mordecai as someone *who spoke up to help the king* (lit. 'who spoke good concerning the king', see NKJV). Mordecai's lasting legacy is that he combined service to the king with service to his people, without compromising on either account. He serves both and speaks up for both, desiring for both their good and their peace.

Meaning

Esther's absence from this chapter is noticeable but not inexplicable. She played her important part in the story by securing Haman's exposure and reversing the circumstances facing the Jews. By eulogizing Mordecai as the symbol of reversal, these final verses, implicitly praise her achievements. Mordecai's status before his king and his people mirrors the definitive moment in Esther's life, where she exposed Haman as enemy of the king and her people (7:6). But whereas Esther had a passing strategic role to play in her people's future, Mordecai's role is on-going. The future of the Jewish people in the Persian world is tied up with Mordecai's ability to hold king and people together. With Mordecai in place the Jews have a mediator; there is someone co-operating with the king with their interests at heart. For this reason their future can be viewed as a positive one. As Bauckham comments, 'In an absolute despotism where so much depends on who has the king's favour, this is how things work' (1989: 127). The significance of this final chapter lies in its commentary on the narrative story-line: it is a story-line that has a present significance. Reversals are possible.

The Jewish people have a future. There will always be another chapter in the on-going story of the survival of God's people. This is a story with a meaning that demands to be remembered, recorded and celebrated.

APPENDIX: THE GREEK ADDITIONS

The 107 additional verses contained in the Greek version of Esther deserve further comment. There are a number of small units of additional text, but there are also six main blocks of text that are not present in the Hebrew manuscripts of Esther. In the Jerusalem Bible, these six blocks of text occur in italics at the appropriate place in the story (following the Septuagint order), but in other Bible texts they are omitted altogether or they are placed in the Apocrypha, removed from their original context. Although the latter position reflects the decision of Jerome that these additions were to be classed as deutero-canonical, their significance and meaning is undermined by their extraction from their original context. This is regrettable because, if these texts have any importance, it must be related to their emergence within the Esther story, as that story emerged within the life of a community of faith. Indeed, many of the features of the Esther story in the Greek additions can be understood only if their emergence within a Greek culture is respected.

It is now commonplace to refer to the additions by letters A–F. The table on page 158 is an attempt to identify the placement, content and features of these six additions according to the Septuagint text:

A quick look at the content column will confirm that the Additions have their own structure. For example, the dream of Addition A is interpreted in Addition F; the text of Haman's edict (Addition B) is mirrored by the text of Mordecai's edict (Addition E). It is also quite clear that the Additions perform a number of roles within the new story that emerges:

- They fill in 'gaps' (e.g. the plot referred to in Addition A supplies a reason for Haman's animosity towards Mordecai and establishes the plot motif at an early point in the narrative).
- They provide a 'frame' for the story (i.e. Mordecai's dream and its interpretation, Addition A(i) and F(i)). Incidentally, this frame, with its apocalyptic features, may intend to establish a new understanding of the genre of Esther.
- They add religious features to the text (e.g. in the form of prayers in Addition C) by the numerous references to God throughout the Additions.
- They develop characterization (e.g. Esther's character is developed in Addition D, her piety in Addition C(ii); Haman is established as the villain at every opportunity – see Additions A and B).
- They bear evidence to the concerns of a Greek world-view (e.g. the Greek pre-occupation with religious identity is perhaps responsible for elements within Esther's prayer, Addition C(ii)).
- They reflect Greek story-telling preferences by adding theatrical elements into a rather abrupt and terse story and by replacing ambiguity with clarity.
- The final inscription commends the story to its community.

	Placement	**Content**	**Features**
Addition A	Inserted before Esth. 1:1	i. Dream of Mordecai ii. Mordecai uncovers a plot	Expressed in apocalyptic language, the dream stresses the importance of God's activity and establishes Mordecai at centre stage. The emphasis is on the instability of the king's court and on Haman's corruption.
Addition B	Inserted before Esth. 3:14	Text of Haman's edict against the Jews	Flamboyant language typical of the Persian court dominates this letter written in the name of the king. Haman's self-obsession is clear (Haman is the author of this edict in which he flatters himself).
Addition C	Inserted before Esth. 5:1	i. Prayer of Mordecai ii. Prayer of Esther	Reflecting the Psalms, these prayers offer to God praise, heart-felt longings and personal cries for justice; they recall God's work in the past and call for his intervention again. Mordecai and Esther's piety emerges.
Addition D	Replaces Esth. 5:1–2, after Addition C	Description of Esther approaching the king	Introduces melodrama through a detailed description of Esther's beauty, coupled with her internal turmoil and physical weakness. The king appears graciously disposed towards Esther.
Addition E	Inserted before Esth. 8:13	Text of Mordecai's edict defending the Jews	Identifying Haman as a Macedonian trying to transfer the Persian Empire to the Macedonians, the edict (written in the name of the king) concentrates on vilifying Haman and praising God.
Addition F	Inserted after Esth. 10:3	i. Mordecai interprets his dream ii. Inscription	The meaning of the apocalyptic dream is related to the events of the Esther story and God is identified as the main player. The unusual feature is that Mordecai is identified as a dragon (traditionally reserved for the enemy of God!). The inscription relates details of those involved in the translation and distribution of the Greek story. It establishes that the book was 'about Purim' and was authentic and trustworthy.

The most significant minor additions in the Greek text of Esther are:

Esther 2:20   Esther is brought up 'to fear God and keep his laws'.
Esther 4:8   Mordecai tells Esther to 'call on the Lord'.
Esther 6:1   'The Lord took sleep from the king' explains his insomnia.
Esther 6:13   'The living God is with him' is part of Zeresh's recognition of Mordecai's strength.

In all these minor additions God is introduced into the narrative, and the God so hidden in the Hebrew text is unambiguously present in the story.

Whatever else may be said, it is clear that to some communities of faith these additions assumed canonical status. For this reason alone, their content cannot be ignored completely. However, like all texts, in order to understand them appropriately, we need to be alert to their origins in order to understand their features. The Greek background has clearly had its effect on the style, content, preoccupations and genre of the Greek Esther story.

THE TEXT OF THE GREEK ADDITIONS[1]

A.

In the second year of the reign of the great King Ahasuerus, on the first day of Nisan, a dream came to Mordecai son of Jair, son of Shimei, son of Kish, of the tribe of Benjamin, a Jew living at Susa and holding high office at the royal court. He was one of the captives whom Nebuchadnezzar, king of Babylon, had deported from Jerusalem with Jeconiah, king of Judah.

This was his dream. There were cries and noise, thunder and earthquakes, and disorder over the whole earth. Then two great dragons came forward, each ready for the fray, and set up a great roar. At the sound of them every nation made ready to wage war against the nation of the just. A day of darkness and gloom, of affliction and distress, oppression and great disturbance on earth! The righteous nation was thrown into consternation at the fear of the evils awaiting them, and prepared for death, crying out to God. Then from their cry, as from a little spring, there grew a great river, a flood of water. Light came as the sun rose, and the humble were raised up and devoured the mighty.

---

1. The text is taken from The Jerusalem Bible, published and copyright 1966, 1967 and 1968 by Darton, Longman & Todd Ltd and Doubleday & Co. Inc., and is used by permission of the publishers.

On awakening from this dream and vision of God's designs, Mordecai thought deeply on the matter, trying his best all day to discover what its meaning might be.

Lodging at court with Bigthan and Teresh, two of the king's eunuchs who guarded the palace, Mordecai got wind of their intentions and uncovered their plot. Learning that they were preparing to assassinate King Ahasuerus, he warned the king against them. The king gave orders for the two eunuchs to be tortured; they confessed and were executed. The king then had these events recorded in his Chronicles, while Mordecai himself also wrote an account of them. The king then appointed Mordecai to an office at court and rewarded him with presents. But Haman son of Hammedatha, the Agagite, who enjoyed high favour with the king, determined to injure Moredecai in revenge for the king's two eunuchs.

B.

The text of the letter was as follows:

'The great King, Ahasuerus, to the governors of the hundred and twenty-seven provinces stretching from India to Ethiopia, and to their subordinate district commissioners.

'Being placed in authority over many nations and ruling the whole world, I have resolved never to be carried away by the insolence of power, but always to rule with moderation and clemency, so as to assure for my subjects a life ever free from storms and, offering my kingdom the benefits of civilisation and free transit from end to end, to restore that peace which all men desire. In consultation with our advisers as to how this aim is to be effected, we have been informed by one of them, eminent among us for prudence and well proved for his unfailing devotion and unshakeable trustworthiness, and in rank second only to our majesty, Haman by name, that there is, mingled among all the tribes of the earth a certain ill-disposed people, opposed by its laws to every other nation and continually defying the royal ordinances, in such a way as to obstruct that form of government assured by us to the general good.

'Considering therefore that this people, unique of its kind, is in complete opposition to all mankind from which it differs by its outlandish system of laws, that it is hostile to our interests and that it commits the most heinous crimes, to the point of endangering the stability of the realm:

'We command that the people designated to you in the letters written by Haman, appointed to watch over our interests and a second father to us, are all, including women and children, to be destroyed root and branch by the swords of their enemies, without any pity or mercy, on the fourteenth day of the twelfth month, Adar, of the present year, so that, these past and present malcontents being in one day forcibly thrown down to Hades, our government may henceforward enjoy perpetual stability and peace.'

C.

Mordecai's prayer
Then calling to mind all the wonderful works of the Lord, he offered this prayer:

> 'Lord, Lord, King and Master of all things,
> everything is subject to your power,
> and there is no one who can withstand you
> in your will to save Israel.

> 'Yes, you have made heaven and earth,
> and all the marvels that are under heaven.
> You are the Lord of all,
> And there is none who can resist you, Lord.

> 'You know all things;
> you know, Lord, you know,
> that no insolence, arrogance, vainglory
> prompted me to this,
> to this refusal to bow down
> before proud Haman.
> I would readily have kissed his feet
> for the safety of Israel.

> 'But what I did, I did
> rather than place the glory of a man

above the glory of God;
and I will not bow down to any
but to you, Lord;
in so refusing I will not act in pride.

'And now, Lord God,
King, God of Abraham,
spare your people!
For men are seeking our ruin
and plan to destroy your ancient heritage.
Do not overlook your inheritance,
which you redeemed for your own out of the land of Egypt.
Hear my supplication,
have mercy on your heritage,
and turn our grief into rejoicing,
that we may live to hymn your name, Lord.
Do not suffer the mouths
of those who praise you to perish.'

And all Israel cried out with all their might, for they were faced with death.

Esther's prayer

Queen Esther also took refuge with the Lord in the mortal peril which had overtaken her. She took off her sumptuous robes and put on sorrowful mourning. Instead of expensive perfumes she covered her head with ashes and dung. She humbled her body severely, and the former scenes of her happiness and elegance were now littered with tresses torn from her hair. She besought the Lord God of Israel in these words:

'My Lord, our King, the only one,
come to my help, for I am alone
and have no helper but you
and am about to take my life in my hands.

'I have been taught from my earliest years, in the bosom of my family,

that you, Lord, chose
Israel out of all the nations
And our ancestors out of all the people of old times
to be your heritage for ever;
and that you have treated them as you promised.

'But then we sinned against you,
and you handed us over to our enemies
for paying honour to their gods.
Lord, you are just.

'But even now they are not satisfied
with the bitterness of our slavery:
they have put their hands in the hands of their idols
to abolish the decree that your own lips have uttered,
to blot out your heritage,
to stop the mouths of those who praise you,
to quench your altar and the glory of your House,
and instead to open the mouths of the heathen.
And sing the praise of worthless idols
And forever to idolise a king of flesh.

'Do not yield your sceptre, Lord,
to non-existent beings.
Never let men mock at our ruin.
Turn their designs against themselves,
And make an example of him who leads the attack on us.
Remember, Lord; reveal yourself
in the time of our distress.

'As for me, give me courage,
King of gods and master of all power.
Put persuasive words into my mouth
when I face the lion;
change his feeling into hatred for our enemy,
that the latter and all like him may be brought to their end.

'As for ourselves, save us by your hand,
and come to my help, for I am alone
and have no one but you, Lord.
You have knowledge of all things,
and you know that I hate honours from the godless,
that I loathe the bed of the uncircumcised,
of any foreigner whatever.
You know I am under constraint,
that I loathe the symbol of my high position
bound round my brow when I appear at court;
I loathe it as if it were a filthy rag
and do not wear it on my days of leisure.
Your handmaid has not eaten at Haman's table,
nor taken pleasure in the royal banquets,
nor drunk the wine of libations.
Nor has your handmaid found pleasure
from the day of her promotion until now
except in you, Lord, God of Abraham.
O God, whose strength prevails over all,
listen to the voice of the desperate,
save us from the hand of the wicked,
and free me from my fear.'

D.

On the third day,[2] when she had finished praying, she took off her suppliant's mourning attire *and dressed herself in her full splendour.* Radiant as she then appeared, she invoked God who watches over all men and saves them. Then she took two maids with her. With a delicate air she leaned on one, while the other accompanied her carrying her train. She leaned on the maid's arm as though languidly, but in fact because her body was too weak to support her; the other maid followed her mistress, lifting her robes which swept the ground. Rosy with the full flush of her beauty, her face radiated joy and love; but her heart shank with fear. *Having passed*

---

2. Italic text denotes words from original Hebrew text.

through door after door, she found herself in the presence of the king. He was
seated on the royal throne, dressed in all his robes of state, glittering
with gold and precious stones – a formidable sight. *Raising his face,*
afire with majesty, he looked on her, blazing with anger. The queen
sank down. She grew faint and the colour drained from her face,
and she leaned her head against the maid who accompanied her.
But God changed the king's heart, *inducing a milder spirit.* He sprang
from his throne in alarm and took her in his arms until she recov-
ered, comforting her with soothing words. 'What is the matter,
Esther?' he said 'I am your brother. Take heart; you will not die;
our order only applies to ordinary people. Come to me.' *And raising
his golden sceptre he laid on her neck,* embraced her and said, 'Speak to
me'. 'My lord,' she said 'you looked to me like an angel of God,
and my heart was moved with fear of your majesty. For you are a
figure of wonder, my lord, and your face is full of graciousness.'
But as she spoke she fell down in a faint. The king was distressed,
and all his attendants tried their best to revive her.

E.

The text of the letter was as follows:

'The great King, Ahasuerus, to the satraps of the hundred and
twenty-seven provinces which stretch from India to Ethiopia, to
the provincial governors and to all our loyal subjects, greeting.

'Many men, repeatedly honoured by the extreme bounty of their
benefactors, only grow the more arrogant. It is not enough for them
to seek our subjects' injury, but unable as they are to support the
weight of their own surfeit they turn to scheming against their benefactors themselves. Not content with banishing gratitude from the
human heart, but elated by the plaudits of men unacquainted with
goodness, notwithstanding that all is for ever under the eye of God,
they vainly expect to escape his justice, so hostile to the wicked.
Thus it has often happened to those placed in authority that, having
entrusted friends with the conduct of affairs and allowed themselves to be influenced by them, they find themselves sharing with
these the guilt of innocent blood and involved in irremediable
misfortunes, the upright intentions of rulers having been misled by
false arguments of the evilly disposed. This may be seen without

recourse to the history of earlier times to which we have referred; you have only to look at what is before you, at the crimes perpetrated by a plague of unworthy officials. For the future we will exert our efforts to assure the tranquillity and peace of the realm for all, by adopting new policies and by always judging matters that are brought to our notice in the most equitable spirit.

'Thus Haman son of Hammedatha, a Macedonian, without a drop of Persian blood and far removed from our goodness, enjoyed our hospitality and was treated by us with the benevolence which we show to every nation, even to the extent of being proclaimed our 'father' and being accorded universally the prostration of respect as second in dignity to the royal throne. But he, unable to keep within his own high rank, schemed to deprive us of our realm and of our life. Furthermore, by tortuous wiles and arguments, he would have had us destroy Mordecai, our saviour and constant benefactor, with Esther the blameless partner of our majesty, and their whole nation besides. He thought by these means to leave us without support and so to transfer the Persian empire to the Macedonians.

'But we find that the Jews, marked out for annihilation by this arch-scoundrel, are not criminals: they are in fact governed by the most just of laws. They are sons of the Most High, the great and living God to whom we and our ancestors owe the continuing prosperity of our realm. You will therefore do well not to act on the letter sent by Haman son of Hammedatha, since their author has been hanged at the gates of Susa with his whole household: a well-earned punishment which God, the ruler of all things, has speedily inflicted on him. Put up copies of this letter everywhere, allow the Jews freedom to observe their own customs, and come to their help against anyone who attacks them on the day originally chosen for their maltreatment, that is the thirteenth day of the twelfth month, which is Adar. For the all-powerful God has made this day a day of joy and not of ruin for his chosen people. Jews, for your part, among your solemn festivals celebrate this as a special day with every kind of feasting, so that now and in the future, for you and for Persians of good will it may commemorate your rescue, and for your enemies may stand as a reminder of their ruin.

'Every city and, more generally, every country, which does not follow these instructions, will be mercilessly devastated with fire and sword, and made not only inaccessible to men but hateful to wild animals and even birds for ever.'

F.

And Mordecai said, 'All this is God's doing. I remember the dream I had about these matters, nothing of which has failed to come true: the little spring that became a river, the light that shone, the sun, the flood of water. Esther is the river – she whom the king married and made queen. The two dragons are Haman and myself. The nations are those that banded together to blot out the name of Jew. The single nation, mine, is Israel, those who cried out to God and were saved. Yes, the Lord has saved his people, the Lord has delivered us from all these evils. God has worked such signs and great wonders as have never happened among the nations.

'Two destinies he appointed, one for his own people, one for the nations at large. And these two destinies were worked out at the hour and time and day laid down by God involving all the nations. In this way God has remembered his people and vindicated his heritage; and for them these days, the fourteenth and fifteenth of the month of Adar, are to be days of assembly, of joy and of gladness before God, through all generations and for ever among his people Israel.'

Colophon

In the fourth year of the reign of Ptolemy and Cleopatra, Dositheus, who affirmed that he was a priest and Levite, and Ptolemy his son brought the foregoing letter concerning the Purim. They maintained it as being authentic, the translation having been made by Lysimachus son of Ptolemy, a member of the Jerusalem community.